WORDPRESS BASICS

Everything you need to know to create a WordPress site

2026, Roy Sahupala

Important Note

The methods and programs in this manual are stated without regard to any patents. They are for amateur and study purposes only. All technical data and programs in this book have been compiled by the author with the greatest care and reproduced after thorough checking. Nevertheless, errors cannot be completely excluded. The publisher is therefore forced to point out that it can assume neither any warranty nor any legal responsibility or any form of liability for consequences arising from erroneous information. The reporting of any errors is always appreciated by the author.

Please be advised that the software and hardware names mentioned in this book as well as the brand names of the companies involved are mostly protected by manufacturer's marks, trademarks or by patent law.

Author: R.E. Sahupala
ISBN/EAN: 979-8-8833-2184-8
First edition: 02-03-2024
Edition: 01-26 KDP
NUR-code: 994
Publisher: WJAC
Website: www.wp-books.com/basics

With special thanks to:
My dear wife Iris van Hattum and our son Ebbo Sahupala.

TABLE OF CONTENTS

INTRODUCTION

Are you interested in creating a professional website independently, even without any technical knowledge, and with content that needs regular updates? If so, a Content Management System (CMS) might be your best bet. There are several CMS options available, with WordPress being one of the most popular.

The decision to choose WordPress depends on various factors. As a web designer, the main appeal for me lies in its user-friendly interface and ease of maintenance. Installing WordPress is quick and simple, making it a hassle-free option for both designers and clients to get started promptly.

When setting up a WordPress site, you have access to numerous free themes to choose from. In this book, I'll walk you through the process of installation, configuration, and management of WordPress. Additionally, I'll demonstrate how to enhance the system by incorporating essential components such as forms, galleries, media features, backups, security measures, and search engine optimization plugins.

For efficient work with WordPress, having a web server on your computer can be beneficial. I'll provide easy-to-follow instructions on how to turn your computer into a web server. Furthermore, I'll explain the process of transferring a WordPress website to an internet server.

This book serves as a solid foundation for delving into WordPress independently. If you're eager to explore further, consider visiting *wordpress.org* for additional resources and insights.

Every exercise presented in this book is practical, focusing solely on the most essential steps while omitting any unnecessary descriptions, ensuring immediate applicability.

For further information, visit **wp-books.com/basics**.
Instructions are provided for both MacOS and Windows users.

Who is this book for?

▸ Individuals interested in independently setting up a WordPress site.
▸ Those seeking independence from developers.
▸ Individuals with no programming background.
▸ Multimedia students.
▸ Web editors.
▸ Anyone aiming to create their own weblog or site.

Tip: Take your time! Carefully read each chapter before sitting down at the computer.

What do you need?

To develop a WordPress site, you'll need the following:

 ▸ A web server or web host
 ▸ The latest version of WordPress
 ▸ An internet browser

You can develop a WordPress site on your computer using a **local web server**. This book provides step-by-step instructions on how to install and utilize a web server on your computer. Once you've developed your Word-Press site, you'll need a **web host** to publish it on the internet.

To provide WordPress with the necessary content, you'll use an **internet browser** to connect to the CMS platform.

It's advisable to install more than one browser, as certain WordPress features may not work optimally in your preferred browser. In such cases, you can quickly switch to another browser.

All exercises in this book have been tested with Firefox, Safari, Google Chrome, and Microsoft Edge. Make sure to always use the latest version of your browser.

Purpose of this book

This book is designed for individuals who want to leverage WordPress quickly and practically, even without technical expertise.

The book covers both Local and Remote installations of WordPress. A local installation offers the advantage of allowing experimentation before publishing the results online.

The book focuses solely on essential explanations, enabling readers to gain sufficient experience with WordPress. Once familiar, readers can further explore the platform independently.

For those interested in delving deeper into WordPress, advanced books are available, such as **WordPress - Advanced, WordPress - Gutenberg, WordPress - Classic Theme**, and **WordPress - Block Theme** (new theme format). Additionally, for creating online stores, there's the book **WordPress - WooCommerce**.

For more information, visit: **wp-books.com**.

SERVER ON YOUR COMPUTER

WordPress is a CMS platform that can be installed directly on the internet. An internet server supporting PHP and MYSQL is necessary for this purpose, a service offered by most web hosts. However, it is recommended to first develop a website on your personal computer before launching it online.

Setting up a WordPress website on your personal computer offers several advantages:

▸ Independence from domain names and web hosting.
▸ Faster production process.
▸ Backup available once the site is online.
▸ Ability to experiment with a local platform before implementing changes on a remote (internet) platform.

Installing WordPress on your personal computer requires the utilization of a scripting language (PHP) and a database (MySQL).

PHP, short for Hypertext Preprocessor, is an open-source, server-side scripting language responsible for the system's operation, acting as the engine of your website.

MySQL manages data storage, including content, settings, and various types of site information.

If you're interested in learning more about PHP and MySQL, there is an abundance of resources and explanations available on the internet.

Installing a web server on your computer may seem complicated at first, but it essentially involves installing a program. Once the program is installed and activated, you can proceed to install and manage WordPress on your computer, where you'll have exclusive access to your WordPress site.

There are several web server programs available, two popular options being **LOCAL** and **MAMP**, which are compatible with both MacOS and Windows.

LOCAL allows you to install WordPress sites exclusively, while MAMP enables the installation of multiple CMS sites, including WordPress.

To get started, open an internet browser and navigate to **localwp.com**. LOCAL also installs Apache, MySQL, and PHP, essential components for running WordPress.

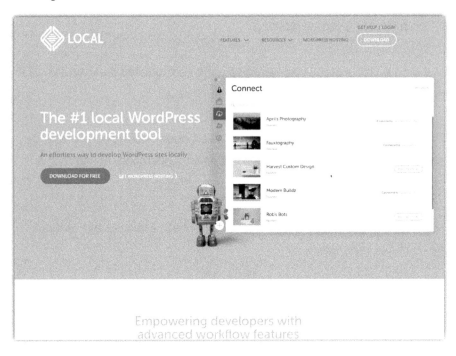

To download LOCAL, follow these steps:

1. Go to the **Downloads** section of the website.
2. A pop-up window will appear. Choose either the **Mac** or **Windows** version based on your operating system.
3. Fill in the required information in the form provided.
4. Click the **GET IT NOW** button.

The following chapters provide detailed instructions on how to install LOCAL and MAMP on both MacOS and Windows computers.

If you already have a web server installed on your computer and are familiar with installing a CMS platform, you can skip directly to the chapter *INSTALLING WORDPRESS ON YOUR COMPUTER*.

Alternatively, if you want to install WordPress directly on the internet, navigate to the chapter *INSTALLING WORDPRESS ON THE INTERNET*.

WEB SERVER FOR MACOS

Before installing LOCAL, please read through this chapter carefully.
Note that the software is not available through the App Store.

Go to **Apps > System Settings > Privacy & Security**.

Activate the option **App Store and identified developers**.

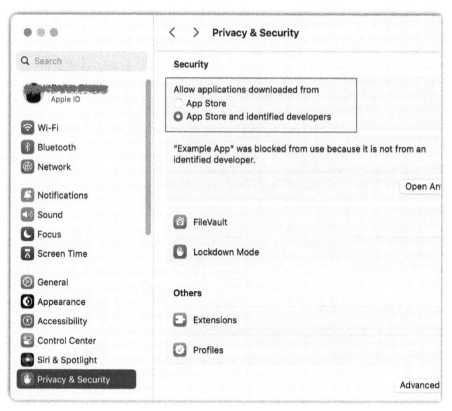

Once this is done, you can proceed with installing LOCAL.

After downloading LOCAL, you'll find a **.dmg** file in your **Downloads** folder.

Double-click on the **local-9.1.0-mac.dmg** file to open it (the version number may vary). A window will appear.

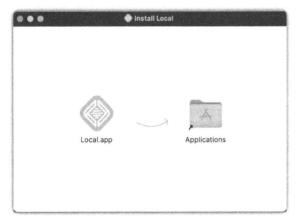

From this window, drag the **Local.app** icon to the **Applications** folder (App folder).

Congratulations! LOCAL is now installed.

Start up LOCAL

Go to **Apps > LOCAL** and launch the program.

You'll be prompted by Finder to grant permission. Click **Open** to proceed.

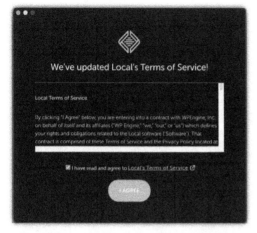

Agree to the terms and conditions and click on **I AGREE**.

A new screen will appear.

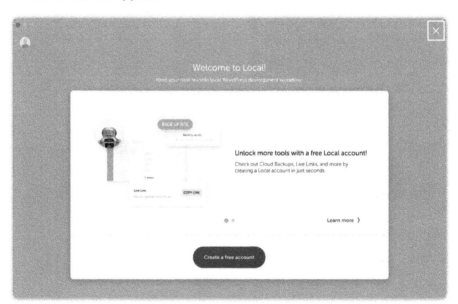

You don't need to create an account. Simply click the white cross at the top right to proceed to the next screen.

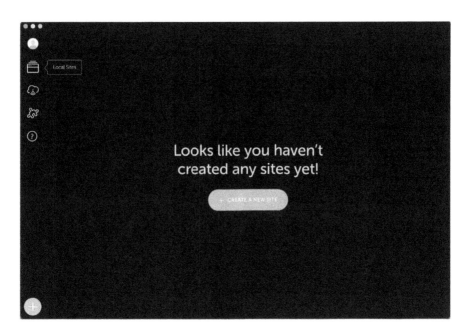

Before proceeding with WordPress installation, close the program by going to **Main Menu > Local > Quit**, or use the key combination **Command+Q**.

Your web server is now installed. In the chapter *INSTALLING WORD-PRESS*, you'll continue with the LOCAL program. If you're interested in learning more about LOCAL, visit *www.localwp.com*.

In case installing LOCAL fails, you can use MAMP as an alternative.
Go to *www.mamp.info.*

1. Download **MAMP & MAMP PRO** for MacOS.
2. Double-click the **.pkg** file in the **Downloads** folder.
3. Follow the installation process.

Tip: After installing MAMP, you have 2 programs *MAMP* and *MAMP PRO.*
The free version can be found in the **Apps folder > MAMP**.

The Pro version requires a license. The chapter *Installing WordPress manually with MAMP* will guide you on installing WordPress using MAMP.

WEB SERVER FOR WINDOWS

Please read through this chapter before installing LOCAL!

Once the software is downloaded, you'll find **LOCAL-9.1.0-windows** in your Downloads folder (the version number may vary). Double-click on the file to proceed.

The window below appears. It doesn't matter what you select.

Then click **Next >**.

This screen displays the installation path. Click on **Install**.

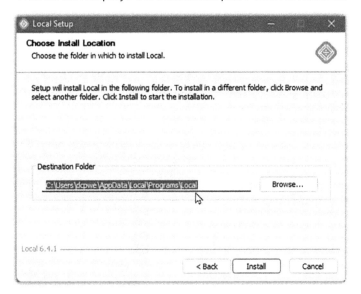

Time for a quick cup of coffee or tea.

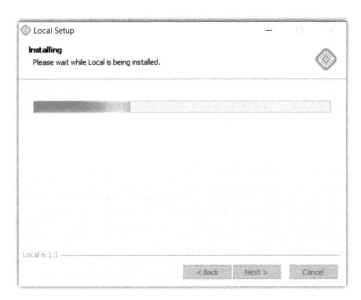

During installation, you may be asked if the program is allowed to make changes to the computer.

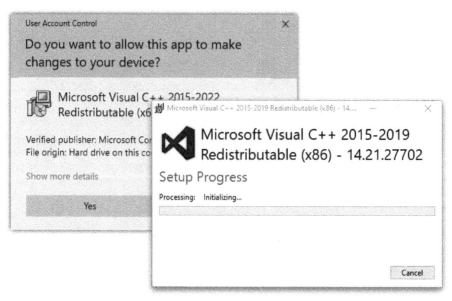

Click **Yes** if prompted. Depending on your Windows version, this process may repeat itself.

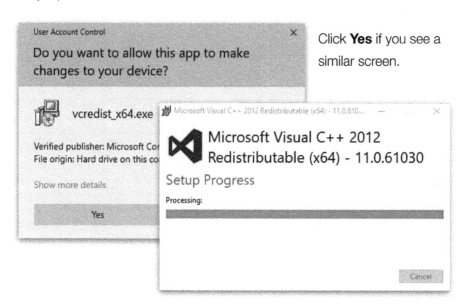

Click **Yes** if you see a similar screen.

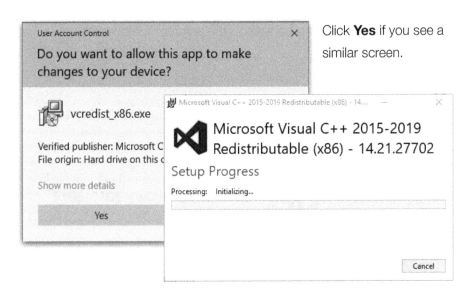

Click **Yes** if you see a similar screen.

Once the installation is complete, you'll see a message.

Congratulations! LOCAL has been successfully installed.

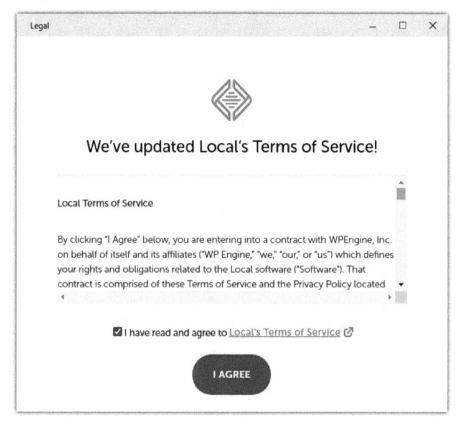

Agree to the terms and conditions by clicking the **I AGREE** button.

If an **Error Reporting** pop-up screen appears, click the **No** button.

LOCAL may ask if you want to create an account, but this is not required. Simply click the white cross at the top right to proceed to the next screen (do not click the cross to exit the program).

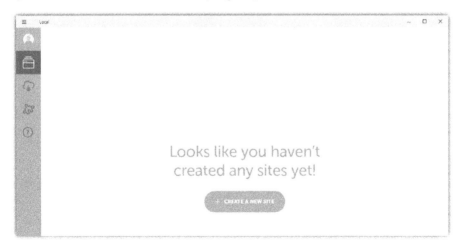

From this window, you can proceed to install WordPress sites. Before do-ing so, close LOCAL.

You can do this by clicking on the cross at the top right or from the main menu: go to **Main Menu > Local > Exit**, or use the key combination **Ctrl+Q**.

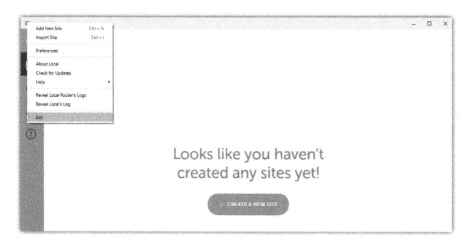

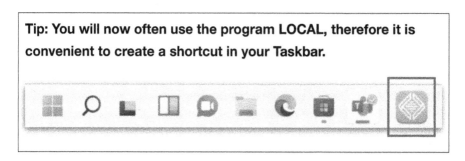

Tip: You will now often use the program LOCAL, therefore it is convenient to create a shortcut in your Taskbar.

Startup LOCAL

Launch the program. Go to **Start**. and find LOCAL under **Recently added**, under the **L** category, or use the **search field**.

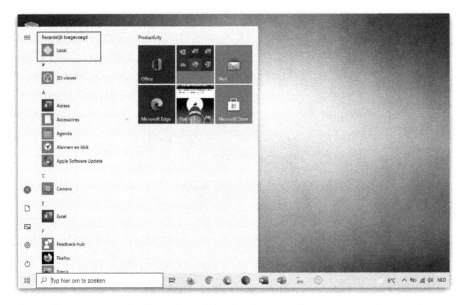

Once the program is started, a LOCAL window will appear, with **Apache**, **PHP**, and **MySQL** activated in the background.

In the next chapter *INSTALL WORDPRESS* you'll continue working with LOCAL.

For more information about the settings and features of LOCAL, visit *www.localwp.com*.

In case installing LOCAL fails, you can use MAMP as an alternative.
Go to *www.mamp.info.*

1. Download **MAMP & MAMP PRO** - Windows.
2. Double-click the **.exe** file in the Downloads folder.
3. Go through the installation process.

Tip: After installing MAMP, you have 2 programs *MAMP* and *MAMP PRO.*

You may use MAMP for free. This can be found in the **Apps folder > MAMP**. A Pro version requires a license. In the chapter *Installing Word-Press manually with MAMP* you'll read how to install WordPress.

INSTALL WORDPRESS

According to WordPress.org:

"WordPress is software designed for everyone, with an emphasis on accessibility, performance, security and ease of use. We believe great software should work with minimal setup, so you can focus on sharing your story, product or services for free. The basic WordPress software is simple and predictable, making it easy to get started. It also offers powerful features for growth and success."

WordPress is an open-source Content Management System (CMS) primarily designed for creating blog sites. Its user-friendly operation and interface have led to its widespread popularity, with WordPress now powering 43% of all websites on the Internet, making it the number one choice among Open Source CMS platforms. At *WordPress.org*, you can find a list of companies and institutions that have adopted this system.

The advantages of WordPress include:

▸ Quick and easy to understand and manage due to its non-technical nature.
▸ Installation can be accomplished within minutes.
▸ Relatively stable and secure.
▸ Continuous development and updates.
▸ Easy upgrades to the latest stable version.
▸ System expansion through plugins, with over 60,042 plugins available at the time of writing.
▸ Thousands of available WordPress themes (templates) that can be quickly changed while maintaining content.
▸ Ability to create custom WordPress themes or modify existing ones with knowledge of HTML and CSS.
▸ Large community providing a vast source of knowledge and support.

As of January 2022, WordPress 5.9 has been released, bringing improvements to the Block Editor, more intuitive interactions, and improved accessibility, among other enhancements. This release also introduces the first Block theme called Twenty Twenty-Two.

While WordPress's focus is on creating blog sites, this book emphasizes setting up a WordPress site quickly and practically. It covers creating a site and utilizing the blogging feature, catering to both informative websites and blog sites.

WordPress on your computer

Installing WordPress on your computer allows you to work independently without relying on a web host. You can achieve this by using programs like **LOCAL** or **MAMP**, both of which are free to use.

There are two methods to install WordPress on your computer:

1. **Automatic** WordPress installation using LOCAL.
2. **Manual** WordPress installation using MAMP.

Automatic WordPress installation with LOCAL

To automatically install WordPress using LOCAL, follow these steps. Note that these instructions are applicable for both Windows and MacOS:

Open the **LOCAL** program.

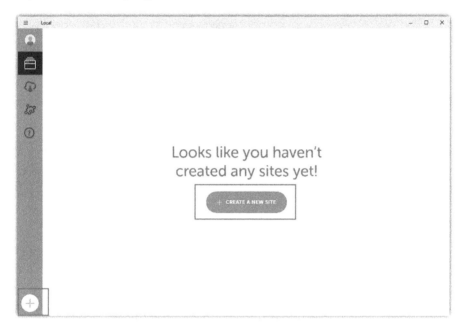

Click on the **+ CREATE A NEW SITE** button or the **+** button at the bottom left of the screen.

Note: During the installation process, your computer system (Windows or MacOS) may ask for permission for Local to make changes. Always grant permission if prompted.

Proceed through the installation process and then click on the **CONTINUE** button.

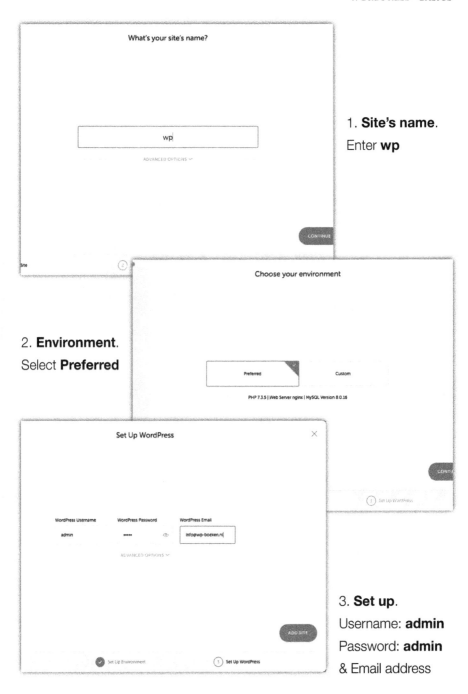

1. Site's name.
Enter **wp**

2. Environment.
Select **Preferred**

3. Set up.
Username: **admin**
Password: **admin**
& Email address

Note: *admin* is chosen as the username and password because this is a local installation, accessible only by you. It's advisable to change the username and password after exporting the site to a web host.

Wait for the WordPress installation to complete.

Your system (Windows or MacOS) may ask for permission to make changes. Always click **Yes** or **OK** if prompted.

After installation, you'll see the site **wp** listed on the left.
Clicking on it will provide an overview of the selected site.

From this screen, you'll find options like:

STOP SITE: Allows you to turn the site *on* or *off*.

Site Title with a link below it **~/Local Sites/wp >**.

This refers to the installation site folder.

The **wp** folder can be found in a Windows or MacOS user folder.

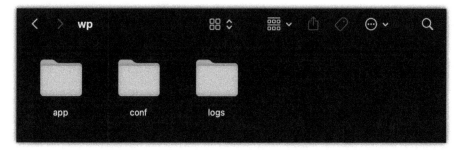

The folder **app > public** contains the WordPress Core files.

3 tabs: **OVERVIEW**, **DATABASE**, and **TOOLS**, providing site information and database access.

OPEN SITE button: Allows you to view the site.

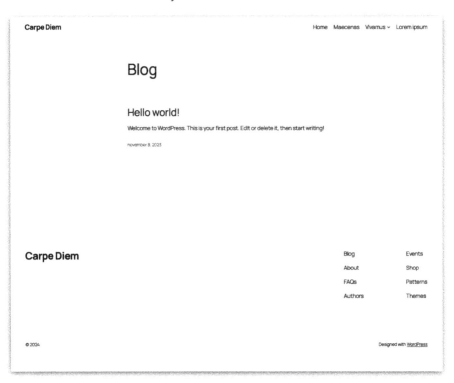

The URL of the site is *wp.local*, indicating it's installed on your computer.

LOCAL installs a default WordPress site, which you can easily customize or convert to another language. In the chapter *BASIC SETTINGS, CONTENT AND ADJUSTMENT* you'll learn how to navigate the WordPress administration section and change the site language.

With the **ADMIN** button you can access the administration section.

Access the administration section by clicking the ADMIN button.
The URL of the admin area is *wp.local/wp-admin*.

You can install WordPress sites as many times as you like.

From the site list, you can use the right mouse button to **Clone**, **Save as Blueprint**, **Rename**, or **Delete** sites.

Tip: Create a Blueprint after changing the site language.

When creating a new site, select **Create from a Blueprint** and choose your **Blueprint**.
There's no need to modify the site language afterward.

For more information about LOCAL settings and features, visit *www.localwp.com*.

Manual WordPress installation with MAMP

For users utilizing a different web server like MAMP, I'll guide you through the process of installing WordPress. While WordPress installation with a web host can be automated or manual, it's recommended for LOCAL users to familiarize themselves with this manual installation method. What is automated with LOCAL needs to be manually executed in this process.

Start **MAMP** (not the PRO version) and click on the **Start** button.

Open the MAMP homepage using the **WebStart** button.

Go to **Tools > phpMyAdmin**.

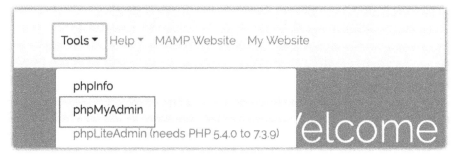

A **phpMyAdmin** window appears. This allows you to create and manage a database. Create a **MySQL** database.

1. Click on the **Databases** tab.

2. Go to **Create new database**.

Give the database a name e.g. **wordpress**.

Click on the **Create** button.

Congratulations! You've created a database. Now, proceed with installing WordPress.

1. Open an Internet browser and go to **wordpress.org**.
Download the latest version of WordPress.

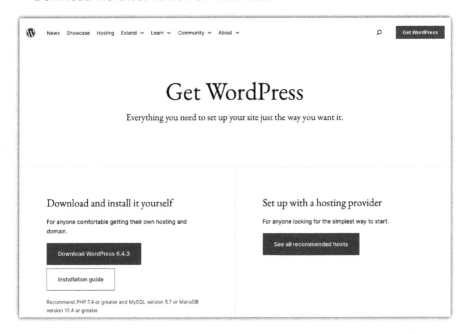

Once downloaded, find the **.zip** file in your **Downloads** folder and unzip
it.

Rename the extracted folder to **wp**.

2. Place the **wp** folder in the root of your server. For MAMP users, this is typically the **htdocs** folder.

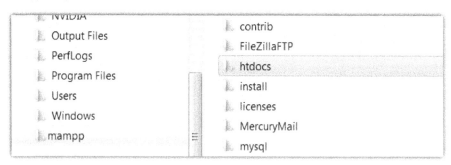

3. Open the MAMP homepage with **WebStart**.
Click on **My Website > wp**.

Or enter the following address in your browser:
http://localhost:8888/wp.

4. Choose your preferred language for the WordPress dashboard and click **Continue**.

5. WordPress will prompt you to have certain information ready.

Welcome to WordPress. Before getting started, we need some information on the database. You will need to know the following items before proceeding.

1. Database name
2. Database username
3. Database password
4. Database host
5. Table prefix (if you want to run more than one WordPress in a single database)

We're going to use this information to create a wp-config.php file. **If for any reason this automatic file creation doesn't work, don't worry. All this does is fill in the database information to a configuration file. You may also simply open wp-config-sample.php in a text editor, fill in your information, and save it as wp-config.php.** Need more help? We got it.

In all likelihood, these items were supplied to you by your Web Host. If you do not have this information, then you will need to contact them before you can continue. If you're all ready...

Let's go!

Click on **Let's get started!**

6. In the provided fields, enter the following information:

Below you should enter your database connection details. If you are not sure about these, contact your host.

Database Name	dbName	The name of the database you want to use with WordPress.
Username	UserName	Your database username.
Password	pwd	Your database password.
Database Host	dbName.mysql.db	You should be able to get this info from your web host, if localhost does not work.
Table Prefix	wp_xxxxxxxxxxxxxxx	If you want to run multiple WordPress installations in a single database, change this.

Submit

Database Name: **wordpress**

Username: **root**   (for MAMP users)

At Password: **root**   (for MAMP users)

Database-host: **localhost**

Tabelprefix: **123wp_** (take note, ends with underscore_)

Click **Submit**.

For MAMP users, the default database username and password are "root, root."

Let's delve a bit deeper into the concept of Table Prefixes in WordPress. It's possible to connect multiple WordPress sites to a single database. This is where the table prefix comes into play during installation. The prefix ensures that each WordPress site retrieves the correct data from the shared database.

By default, WordPress assigns the prefix **wp_** to its tables. However, this default prefix is widely recognized by hackers. To bolster security, it's prudent to modify this default prefix during installation. Opt for a unique prefix, such as **123wp_** (remember to append an underscore afterward).

7. A new window appears.

All right, sparky! You've made it through this part of the installation. WordPress can now communicate with your database. If you are ready, time now to...

Run the installation

Click **Run the installation**.

8. The following window appears.

Site title:	Title of your site
Username:	admin
Password:	admin (You can change this again later)
Confirm password:	Confirm
Email address:	Your email address
Search Engine... :	Do not activate yet

Welcome

Welcome to the famous five-minute WordPress installation process! Just fill in the information below and you'll be on your way to using the most extendable and powerful personal publishing platform in the world.

Information needed

Please provide the following information. Do not worry, you can always change these settings later.

Site Title

My Wordpress Website

Username

AdminWPUser

Usernames can have only alphanumeric characters, spaces, underscores, hyphens, periods, and the @ symbol.

Password

YourPWDAdminUser   Hide

Strong

Important: You will need this password to log in. Please store it in a secure location.

Your Email

your.email@adress.tld

Double-check your email address before continuing.

Search engine visibility

☐ Discourage search engines from indexing this site

It is up to search engines to honor this request.

Install WordPress

9. Click **Install WordPress**.

10. Congratulations! WordPress is now installed. Click **Login**.

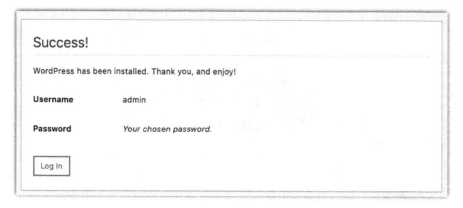

11. Use **admin** for both the username and password and click **Login**.

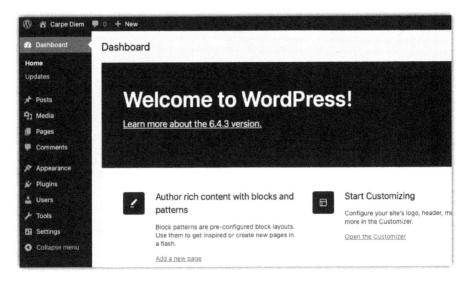

12. In the WordPress admin section, you can configure your site further. Proceed to the Chapter, *WORDPRESS SETTINGS*, for more instructions.

13. To access your site, go to top left, **Visit Site** ore visit the URL: **http://localhost:8888/wp**.

14. To log out of the admin section, click on **Howdy, admin** at the top right and choose **Log Out**.

Carpe Diem   Home   Maecenas   Vivamus ˅   Lorem ipsum

Blog

Hello world!

Welcome to WordPress. This is your first post. Edit or delete it, then start writing!

november 8, 2023

Carpe Diem

Blog   Events

About   Shop

FAQs   Patterns

Authors   Themes

© 2024   Designed with WordPress

INSTALL WORDPRESS ON THE INTERNET

Installing WordPress on the Internet follows the same process as installing it on your computer (refer to the chapter *Installing WordPress*). However, for an online installation, you'll need a **domain name** and **web hosting**, which you can obtain from a hosting provider.

Ensure that your web host supports **PHP** (version 8.3 or higher) and **MySQL** (version 8.0 or higher) before proceeding. Once you have chosen a suitable host, you can begin the installation process. If you haven't selected a domain or hosting yet, you can consider providers like *ionos.com.*

IONOS

After signing up for a domain name and web hosting, you'll receive the necessary information. If you're unsure about database creation or access to phpMyAdmin, contact your web hosting provider. Here are some questions to ask:

▸ Can I install WordPress using an application installer?
▸ If not, is there a database available, and what is its name?
▸ What is the username for my database?
▸ What is the database password?
▸ How do I access phpMyAdmin?

Setting up a **database** and finding **phpMyAdmin** can be challenging for online WordPress installations compared to using LOCAL or MAMP, as you depend on your hosting provider.

Although most Web hosts provide extensive documentation on database management, reaching out to a help desk can speed up the process.

It's important to note that database hosting doesn't always imply that a database has been created for you. Your hosting provider may have already created one, or you may need to create it yourself.

In the following chapters, I'll describe two installation methods:

Wordpress installation **WITH** an app installer, **Method 1**.
Wordpress installation **WITHOUT** an app installer, **Method 2**.

Additionally, in the chapter *MIGRATING A LOCAL SITE TO THE INTERNET*, I'll explain how to transfer a WordPress site from your computer to the Internet, moving it from a **local** environment to a **remote** one.

WordPress installation with an app installer, method 1

Many web hosts provide a control panel with an application installer, simplifying the installation process of CMS platforms like WordPress within minutes and without requiring technical expertise.

1. Log in to your **IONOS** account and navigate to **Menu > Websites & Stores**.

2. Click on **Popular Open-Source solutions**.

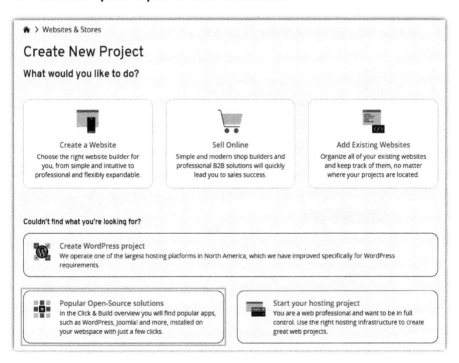

3. On the **Click & Build Overview** page you'll find a list of available applications. Locate **WordPress** and click on **Install**.

4. Choose **Manage WordPress yourself**.

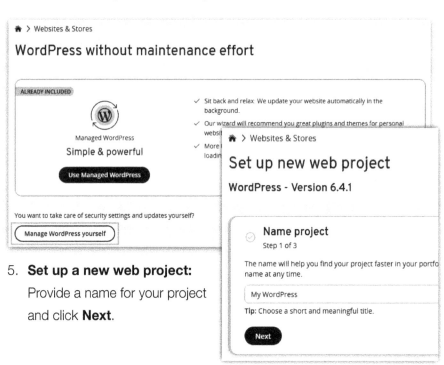

5. **Set up a new web project:**
   Provide a name for your project and click **Next**.

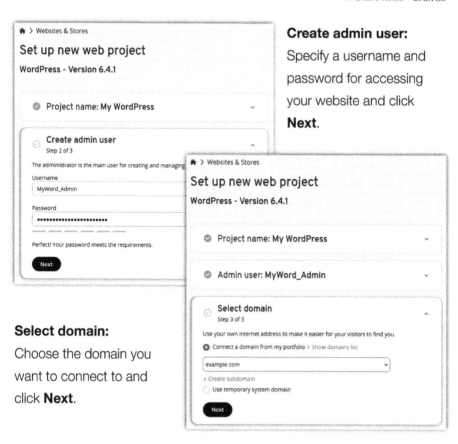

Create admin user:
Specify a username and password for accessing your website and click **Next**.

Select domain:
Choose the domain you want to connect to and click **Next**.

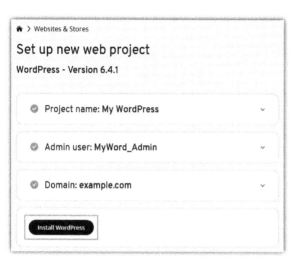

Start the installation, click on **Install WordPress**.

Once the installation is complete, you'll receive an email notification.

WordPress installation without an app installer, method 2

Your web host has provided you with the following (fictitious) data:

```
Technical information for http://www.your_site.com

WWW:
Homepage url:          http://www.your_site.com

CONTROL PANEL
Url:                   https://www.your_site.com:8443
Username:              your_site.com
Password:              1abCdeFg

FTP:
To transfer your website to our server, you will need an
FTP program.

Host:                  ftp.your_site.com
Username:              your_username
Password:              2abCdeFg

EMAIL:
POP3 server:           pop.your_site.com
SMTP server:           http://www.your_host.com/n5
Webmail:               http://www.your_host.com

STATISTICS:
Url:                   https://www.your_host.com/st
User name:             your_site.com
Password:              3abCdeFg
```

In this case, you'll need to create a **database** first before installing Word-
Press. This process typically involves using a **control panel**, where you
can manage various aspects of your site, including creating databases.

Important details provided by your web host include **FTP information** and access to the **control panel**, where you can handle site-related tasks such as managing email addresses and creating databases.

Below you can see a similar control panel called **Plesk**.

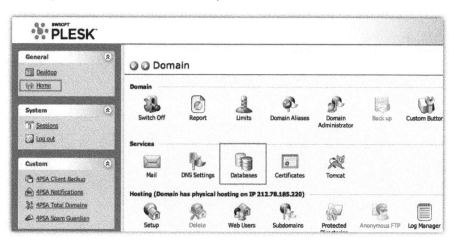

Creating a database can differ between web hosts, but the essential step is that you'll need to create a database yourself from the control panel. The objective is to locate a **database icon** or option within the control panel interface. Typically, you'll find a link to phpMyAdmin, a tool for managing MySQL databases, which will be activated and visible.

While the following explanation assumes a Plesk environment, if your web host doesn't use Plesk, the described method can still provide you with an understanding of what to look for. The process of creating a database is generally similar across different control panel interfaces.

1. Open a web browser and navigate to your **control panel** URL (link) provided by your web host. Log in using your web host credentials.

2. Once logged in, click on **Home** or navigate to your **domain name**, then find and click on **Databases**.

3. Within the Databases section, locate and click on **Add New Database**.

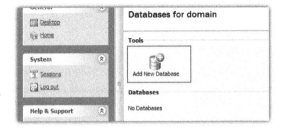

4. In the **Database name** field, specify a desired name for your database. Make sure the Type is set to **MySQL**. Then, click **OK**.

5. Next, create a database user by clicking on **Add New Database User**.

6. In the **Database user name** field, enter a username for the database user. Then, in the **New Password** and **Confirm Password** fields, enter a password for the user. Click **OK** to save the user details.

7. Your database has now been created. Click on **DB WebAdmin** to access the online phpMy-Admin interface in a new window.

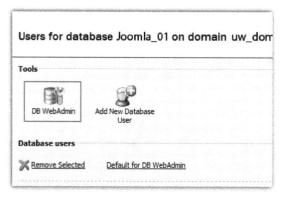

8. Once you've accessed phpMyAdmin, you can log out of your control panel.

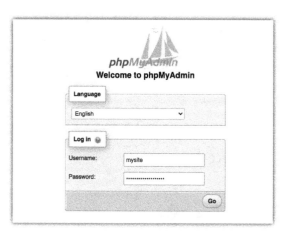

With the database created, you can proceed to install WordPress. Navigate to your website's domain and go through all the installation steps (1 through 11) provided by the WordPress installation wizard.

Here are the essential details you'll need:

▸ FTP information.

▸ MySQL information.

▸ URL address to phpMyAdmin.

Download the latest version of WordPress. **Upload** the extracted contents of the WordPress folder directly into the root directory of your server space. Use an FTP program for this task.

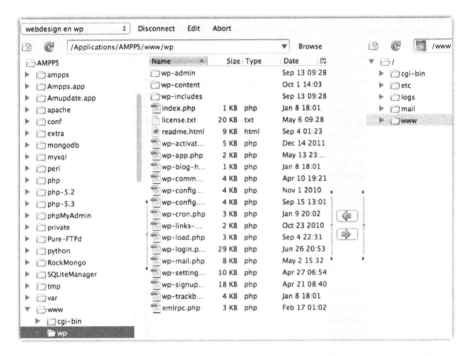

Once the WordPress content is uploaded to your web host, you can initiate the site installation.

1. Open a web browser and navigate to:
   http://www.your_site.com/wp-admin.

2. Choose your preferred language for the WordPress dashboard, then click **Continue**.

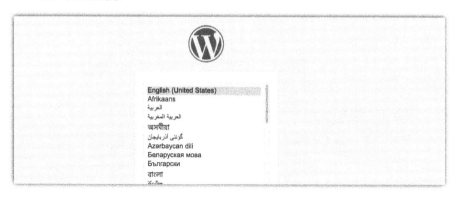

WordPress will prompt you to have certain information on hand to proceed with the installation. This information will be required in the following steps.

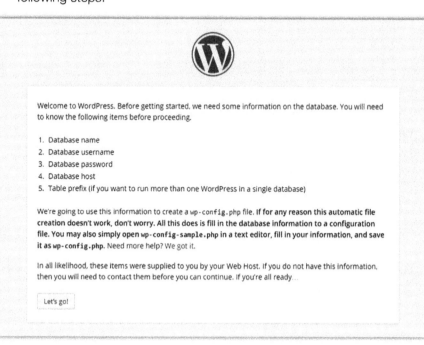

Click on **Let's go!**

3. You'll encounter the window below. Make sure to use your web host data:

Below you should enter your database connection details. If you are not sure about these, contact your host.

Database Name	dbName	The name of the database you want to use with WordPress.
Username	UserName	Your database username.
Password	pwd	Your database password.
Database Host	dbName.mysql.db	You should be able to get this info from your web host, if localhost does not work.
Table Prefix	wp_xxxxxxxxxxxxxxx	If you want to run multiple WordPress installations in a single database, change this.

Submit

Database name:	Name_database (web host data)
Username:	Username_database (web host data)
Password:	Password_database (web host data)
Host name:	Localhost
Tableprefix:	E.g. 123wp_ (note with underscore_)

Click **Submit**.

By default, WordPress assigns the prefix **wp_** to its tables. However, this default prefix is widely recognized by hackers. To bolster security, it's prudent to modify this default prefix during installation. Opt for a unique prefix, such as **123wp_** (remember to append an underscore afterward).

4. A new window appears. Click **Run the installation.**

All right, sparky! You've made it through this part of the installation. WordPress can now communicate with your database. If you are ready, time now to...

Run the installation

5. A new window will appear. Fill in the requested information:

Site title:	Title of your site
Username:	Admin
Password:	Admin (you can change this later)
Email address:	Your email address
Search engine... :	Do not activate yet

Welcome

Welcome to the famous five-minute WordPress installation process! Just fill in the information below and you'll be on your way to using the most extendable and powerful personal publishing platform in the world.

Information needed

Please provide the following information. Do not worry, you can always change these settings later.

Site Title

My Wordpress Website

Username

AdminWPUser

Usernames can have only alphanumeric characters, spaces, underscores, hyphens, periods, and the @ symbol.

Password

YourPWDAdminUser   Hide

Strong

Important: You will need this password to log in. Please store it in a secure location.

Your Email

your.email@adress.tld

Double-check your email address before continuing.

Search engine visibility

☐ Discourage search engines from indexing this site

It is up to search engines to honor this request.

Install WordPress

6. Next, click **Install WordPress**.

7. Congratulations! WordPress is now installed.
   Click **Login** to configure and set up your site.

8. To visit your site, go to the top left and click **Visit Site**.

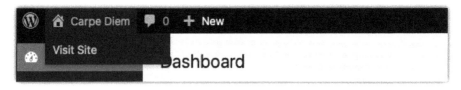

9. To log out, click on **Howdy, admin** at the top right corner and choose **Log Out**.

To access phpMyAdmin, use the following details provided by your web host:

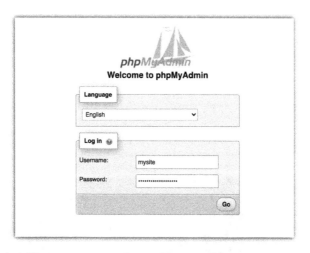

phpMyAdmin URL:	http://phpMyAdmin.your_site.com
Username:	your_phpMyAdmin_username
Password:	your_ phpMyAdmin_password

BASIC SETTINGS, CONTENT AND CUSTOMIZATION

Adding content and customizing a WordPress site will provide you with a clear understanding of how to interact with this system. In this chapter, I cover the following components:

- Viewing the Site.
- **Updating** a WordPress Site.
- Installing the **Twenty Twenty-One** theme.
- Customizing the **Site Title** and **Description**.
- Customizing the **Site Language**.
- Creating Content for the Site: **Posts** and **Pages**.
- Creating a new **Homepage**.
- Creating a **Menu**.
- Using the **Media Library**.
- Adding **Images**.
- Customizing and Creating a **Category**.
- Adding **Widgets** to the site.
- Customizing **footer** information.
- Adding **users**.

Please note: This book uses **WordPress 6.9** and the **Twenty Twenty-One** theme.

After a WordPress installation, the default **Twenty Twenty-Five** theme is displayed. With this, WordPress aims to introduce a new feature called **Full Site Editing**, enabling users to visually modify a **Block Theme**.

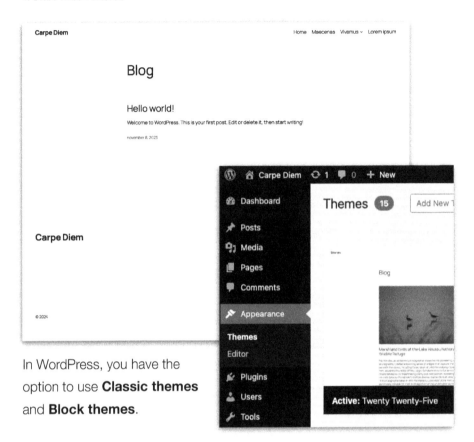

In WordPress, you have the option to use **Classic themes** and **Block themes**.

Since there are currently more Classic themes available (22,000+) than Block themes (1,000+), this book uses the Twenty Twenty-One Classic theme to provide a comprehensive understanding of the platform.

For further details on Block themes, refer to the chapter *BLOCK THEMES* and consult the book **WordPress Block Theme**.

In the chapter *Install Twenty Twenty-One Theme*, you'll learn how to replace the Block theme.

WordPress frontend

To view the frontend of your WordPress website, open a web browser and navigate to your website's URL. If you have WordPress installed locally on your computer, you can start the **LOCAL** or **MAMP** server and access the site.

If using **LOCAL**, click on **OPEN SITE** for the website named **wp**.

For **MAMP**, go to the homepage and click on **My Website > wp**.

In this screen, you'll see all the folders contained within the **MAMP** root directory. Locate and click on the folder named **wp/** to access your WordPress site, which will then open in your web browser.

You have entered the back end of the system. Here you will find a home page showing general information. This page is called "Welcome to WordPress!".

CARPE DIEM

Hello world!

Welcome to WordPress. This is your first post. Edit or delete it, then start writing!

Published February 16, 2024 Edit
Categorized as Uncategorized

Search

| | Search |

Recent Posts

Hello world!

Recent Comments

A WordPress Commenter on Hello world!

Archives

February 2024

Categories

Uncategorized

CARPE DIEM

Proudly powered by WordPress.

- ▸ Site title and Site description (located at the top).
- ▸ Navigation (at the top right, if activated).
- ▸ Default Blog post titled "Hello World!".
- ▸ Widgets such as a search box, most recent posts.
- ▸ Footer section at the bottom.

The presence of widgets on your site may vary depending on your web host's settings. Widgets are customizable site elements like search boxes or archives, which can be added or removed as needed.

The Twenty Twenty-One theme is designed to be responsive, meaning it adapts seamlessly to different screen sizes, making it suitable for viewing on computers, tablets, and smartphones.

This responsive design feature ensures a consistent user experience across various devices.

While WordPress is often associated with blogging, it's also capable of creating and managing informative pages, which is a common use case for many websites. As a web designer, you'll often be tasked with setting up informative WordPress sites, with blogging features being secondary.

In the next chapter, you'll learn how to customize, enhance, or disable specific components within WordPress. Additionally, you'll discover how to create posts, pages, and menus to further customize your site.

WordPress backend

In this chapter, we'll explore the backend of WordPress. To access it, open an internet browser and use one of the following addresses:

For LOCAL installation: http://wp.local/wp-login.php
For MAMP installation: http://localhost:8888/wp/wp-login.php
For online installation: http://www.your_website.com/wp-login.php

Using **wp-login.php** will always redirect you to the backend login page. Remember this link in case you don't have a direct login link.

Upon logging in, you'll encounter the following:

Use login credentials:
- Username = e.g. **admin**
- Password = e.g. **admin**
- Click on **login**

Welcome to WordPress!

You've entered the backend of the system, where you'll find a homepage displaying general information. This page is called the **Dashboard**. Here, you'll stay informed about the latest developments related to your site.

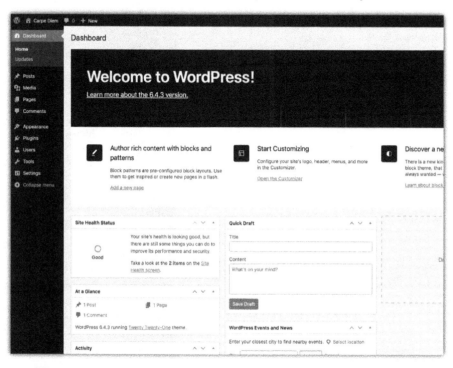

In the left column, you'll find various options that enable you to customize the system and add essential content to your site.

To log out, go to the top right corner. Click on **Howdy, admin** and select **Log Out**.

Dashboard

The menu in WordPress is referred to as the **Dashboard**. It is divided into three main sections:

Section 1:
Home and **Updates**.

Section 2:
Options for adding content to the system, including: **Posts**, **Media**, **Pages**, and **Comments**.

Section 3:
Options for customizing or configuring the system, such as: **Appearance**, **Plugins**, **Users**, **Tools**, and **Settings**.

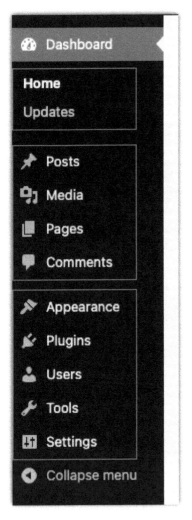

WordPress Updates

After installing WordPress, it's important to keep the system up to date to enhance its security and stability. This includes updating not only the **WordPress core** but also **plugins** and **themes**.

In the Dashboard menu, you'll notice a number displayed next to the word **Updates**, indicating the available updates. Similarly, the number next to **Plugins** indicates the number of plugin updates available.

To check for updates, click on **Updates**. You'll be directed to a screen where you can review available updates.

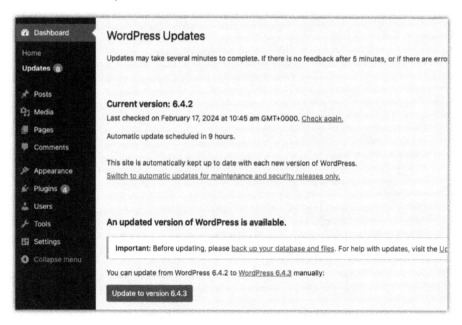

If a new version of WordPress is available, click the **Update WordPress** button. Note, from version 3.7, WordPress can automatically update itself.

If there are updates available for plugins or themes, you can select the specific ones you want to update and then click the respective **Update Plugins** or **Update Themes** button.

Regularly applying updates is crucial as it helps protect your system from security vulnerabilities, resolves any existing issues, and provides access to new features and improvements.

Install Theme Twenty Twenty-One

Go to **Dashboard > Appearance > Themes**.

Click on the **Add new theme** button.

In the search field, type **Twenty Twenty one**.

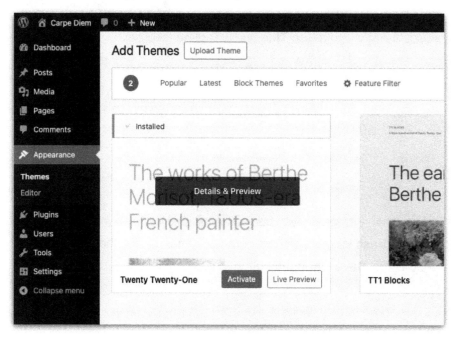

Once the theme appears in the search results, click on the **Install** button. After the installation is complete, click on the **Activate** button.

Now you have successfully installed and activated the classic *Twenty Twenty-One* theme.

If you want to learn more about working with a Block Theme, refer to the chapter *Block Theme.*

Site title and subtitle

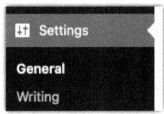

Navigate to:

Dashboard > Settings > General.

In the **General Settings** screen, you can

provide the site with a **Site Title** and a **Tagline** (subtitle).

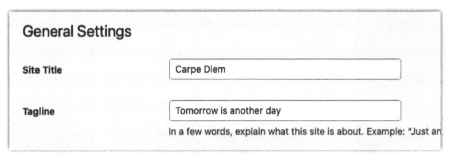

Further down the screen, you can edit additional information including an **email address** for management purposes. After making the desired changes, click the **Save Changes** button to save your settings.

Site language

To change the site language:

Go to **Dashboard > Settings > General - Site Language**.

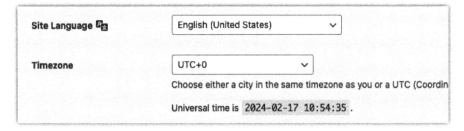

Select your preferred language, then click the **Save Changes** button.

Permalinks

Permalinks in WordPress determine the structure of your website's URLs, which are displayed in your browser's address bar. By default, WordPress uses the "Plain" permalink setting.

To check or change your permalinks settings:
Go to **Dashboard > Settings > Permalinks**.

By default, the **Plain** Permalink structure might be activated, resulting in URLs for new pages or posts with additions like **/?p=123** in the address.

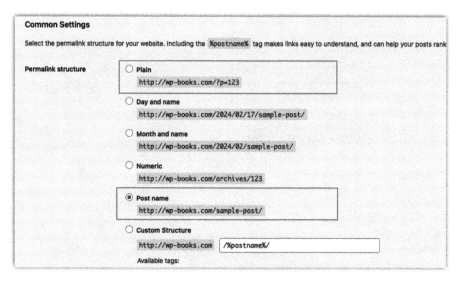

It's advisable to include the post **title** in the URL for clarity to both users and search engines. To include the post or page title in the URL, select **Post name** as the Permalink setting.

Remember to **save** your changes after selecting the desired permalink structure.

Display name

After installing a WordPress site, the **Username** is also used as the **Display Name**, which is publicly shown on the website. This can be visible both in the **Dashboard** and in **published Posts**, revealing half of the login information.

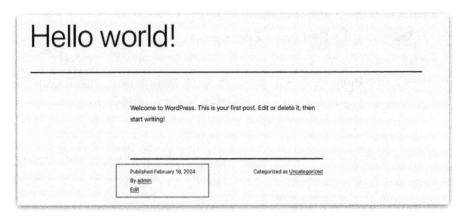

Fortunately, you can change this easily.

Go to **Dashboard > Users - admin**.

Replace the **Nickname** *admin* with *your preferred display name*.

At **Display name publicly as** select - *your preferred display name*.

Note that the **Username** remains unchanged.

Click the **Update Profile** button to save your changes.

View site

To see the outcome of your site, navigate to the menu bar at the top left of the screen:

Site Title (Carpe Diem) > Visit Site.

To return to the Dashboard, once again, use the menu bar at the top left of the screen: **Site Title (Carpe diem) > Dashboard**.

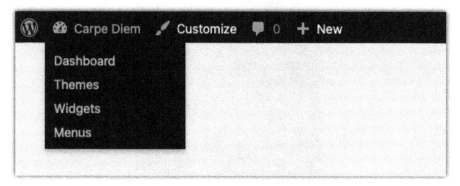

POSTS AND PAGES

In WordPress, you can create both **Posts** and **Pages**, each serving different purposes. Here's the difference.

Posts are like news items or articles that visitors can interact with by leaving comments. They are displayed in chronological order, with the latest post at the top. It can be categorized to organize content effectively.

By default, the homepage of a WordPress website displays a series of blog posts. Posts can be archived by month or category, making it easier for visitors to find specific content.

Pages contain static, timeless information such as About Us, Contact, or Services pages. Unlike posts, they are not stored chronologically and typically do not have comment sections. Although visitors can interact with pages through comment fields if enabled, this functionality is not commonly used for pages. Pages cannot be categorized like posts and are usually accessed through a link or menu.

CARPE DIEM

Sample Page

This is an example page. It's different from a blog post because it will stay in one place and will show up in your site navigation (in most themes). Most people start with an About page that introduces them to potential site visitors. It might say something like this:

" Hi there! I'm a bike messenger by day, aspiring actor by night, and this is my website. I live in Los Angeles, have a great dog

Add Post

1. Go to **Dashboard > Posts > Add New Post**.
2. Provide the post with a **title** and **text**.
   Use the options menu (three dots) to manage blocks, such as deleting them.

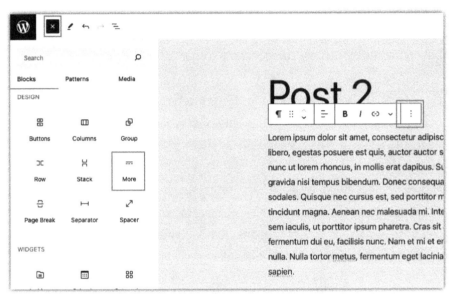

3. Click the ➕ icon at the top left and select **Design > More**.
   A **READ MORE** block appears.

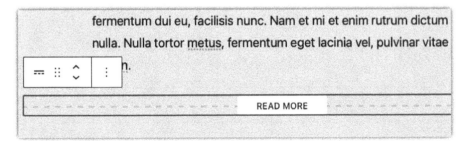

4. Use the options menu, select **Options > Add After** or the ➕ icon to add a **Paragraph** block.

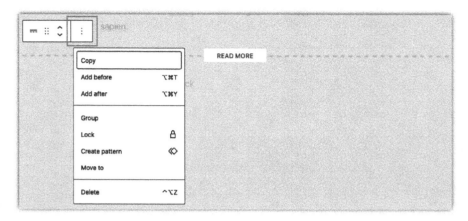

5. Then click the **Publish** button.

6. Click on the WordPress icon (**W** at the top left) and visit the site.
    As you can see, the latest post is at the top of the homepage.

Post 2

Lorem ipsum dolor sit amet, consectetur adipiscing elit. Fusce diam libero, egestas posuere est quis, auctor auctor sem. In accumsan nunc ut lorem rhoncus, in mollis erat dapibus. Suspendisse id odio gravida nisi tempus bibendum. Donec consequat dui at ullamcorper sodales. Quisque nec cursus est, sed porttitor metus. Quisque non tincidunt magna. Aenean nec malesuada... Continue reading

Published February 17, 2024 Edit
Categorized as Uncategorized

The latest post in this case shows the first paragraph.

Click on **Continue reading**.

You will now see the full post with a comment form below.

Before you **publish** a post, there are other options you can use.

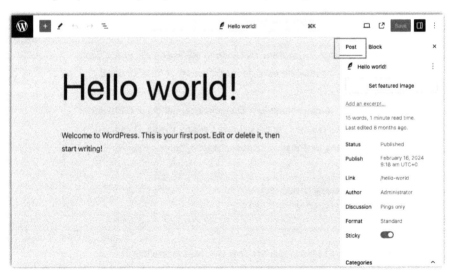

Using the **Post** tab (top right) various options are displayed. If you select a paragraph, **Block** options become visible. The next page shows an overview of all **Post** settings.

Set featured image

Include an image that represents the content of the post.

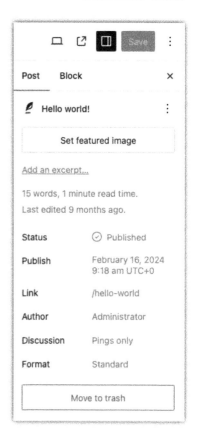

Add an excerpt...

Provide a short summary of the post content.

Status

Select the status and visibility of the post. Sticky, displays the post in a prominent place at the top of the home or blog page.

Publish

Set publication date and sticky option.

Link

Customize the last part of the URL.

Author

Select the author of the post

Discussion

Enable or disable comments and trackbacks for the post.

Format

Allows you to display a message differently. This is theme dependent.

Move to trash

Moves the post to trash.

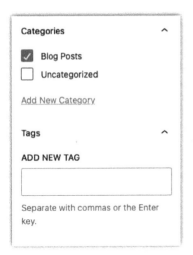

Categories

Organize posts into categories for easier navigation.

Tags

Add keywords to help users and search engines find the post.

For more advanced options and to disable the response form for all new posts, refer to the chapter *Disable Response Form*.

BLOCK EDITOR

WordPress version 5.0, introduced in November 2018, features a new content editor called Gutenberg. As demonstrated in the *Add Post* chapter, you can directly insert a title and text into a post using this editor.

To edit a block within Gutenberg, you first select the block you want to modify, such as a paragraph. This action activates the **Block** tab in the right-hand column. Here, you can adjust the properties of the block using the available **Block Options**, which vary depending on the block type.

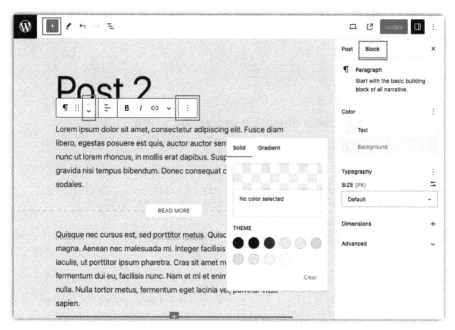

Additionally, you can perform various actions on a block, such as deleting it, by clicking on the **Options menu** represented by **three dots**. You can also adjust the order of blocks using the **Arrow icons**.

By clicking on the ❎ icon you can add **Blocks**, **Patterns** and **Media**.

Block elements are various components such as **text**, **images**, **read more**, **buttons**, **videos**, **music player**, **widgets**, **tables**, and more. These elements are categorized under Text, Media, Design, Widgets, Theme, and Inclusions. You can explore additional block elements by scrolling down the Blocks window or by using plugins to add more options.

Patterns provide a quick way to format a page by combining several block elements into predefined layouts.

The **Media** option allows you to add media from **Openverse** (visit *openverse.org* for more information).

Block-based editing provides users with greater flexibility in formatting a page compared to the classic editor. In the *Image Placement* chapter, you'll learn how to align images with text using block-based editing.

Add Pages

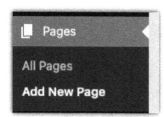

1. Go to **Dashboard > Pages > Add New Page**.
2. Provide a **title** and add **text** to the page.

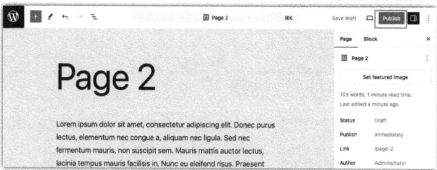

3. Once you're done, click on the **Publish** button twice. After publishing, you can view the page by clicking on the **View Page** button.

If you need to make further edits, you can click on the **Edit Page** button to return.

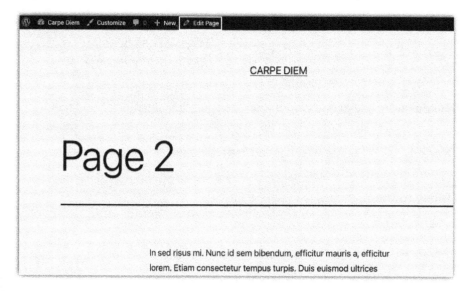

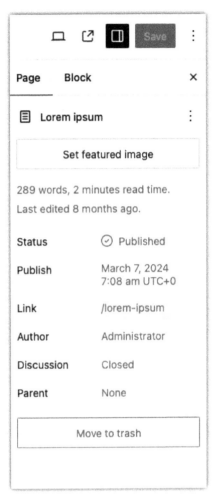

Click on the **Page** tab. Similar to Posts, you'll find options specific to pages that you can apply.

Set featured image, include an image that represents the page content.

Status, here you can set publishing options.

Publish, set the publication date.

Link, the title is automatically included in the last part of the URL.

Author, select the author.

Template, is visible depending on the theme you have. It allows you to choose a specific layout for the page (e.g. *With sidebar* or *Homepage*).

Discussion, in this section you can configure the settings for comments.

Parent, specify under which menu item the page should be placed.

Move to trash, moves the page to trash.

Creating a link

Open the page or post where you want to create the link. Select the text that you want to turn into a link. Click on the **link icon** in the top toolbar. In the Link field, enter the URL and click **Enter**.

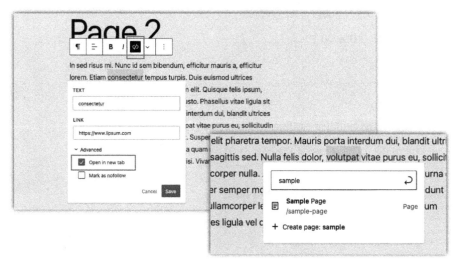

Alternatively, if you want to link to an internal page or post, begin typing the title of the Page/Post, and WordPress will display a list of matching documents. Select the desired Page or Post from the list.

You want the link to open in a new tab, make sure the **Open in new tab** option is activated. You can edit the link by selecting it and then toggling the option.

Finally, save or update the page or post to apply the changes.

Assignment

To gain a sense of how a WordPress site operates, it's useful to set up some **Pages** and **Posts** beforehand.

Begin by creating several Pages with the titles:
- Welcome (front page).
- Who.
- What.
- Where.
- Contact (to be later outfitted with a contact form).
- News (to function as a page summarizing Posts).

Additionally, create Posts with the titles:
- Latest news.
- Weather.

In the next chapter *Customize homepage*, I'll demonstrate how to modify the Homepage.

Likewise, in the *Customize Posts page* chapter, I'll illustrate how to showcase Posts within a designated page titled News.

Lastly, within the *Menu* chapter, I'll guide you through navigating your site using a menu.

Customize homepage

After a default WordPress installation, the Homepage displays an overview of your latest Posts.

If you prefer to start with a specific Page rather than Posts, you can customize this by navigating to: **Dashboard > Settings > Reading**.

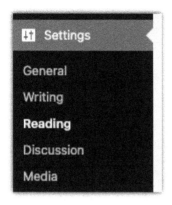

Under **Your homepage displays**, opt for **A static page** instead of **Your latest posts**.

For example, select a static Page.

Choose **Welcome** as the Homepage.

Click **Save Changes** and then view the site to see the updates.

Customize Posts page

If you wish to use your latest posts but not as your homepage, you can achieve this by configuring the **Posts page** option.

Reading Settings

Your homepage displays
- ○ Your latest posts
- ⦿ A static page (select below)

Homepage: Welcome ⌄

Posts page: News ⌄

Blog pages show at most   10 ⌄ posts

Under **Posts page**, select an existing page (e.g., News). When the News page is accessed, all the latest posts are displayed sequentially.

You can specify the number of posts displayed on the page using the **Blog pages show at most** option. Additional posts are archived, and users can access them using an **Archive widget**.

After making your selections, click **Save changes** and then view the site to see the updates.

Before implementing this, it's advisable to create a page with an appropriate title, such as *News* or *Blog*. This page doesn't require any text. Additionally, ensure that the News page is included in the menu structure, as explained in the *Menu* chapter.

Sticky posts

Marking a post as sticky ensures that it remains at the top of a Post page. If your theme supports this feature, the sticky post may also be displayed prominently on the homepage (refer to the *CUSTOMIZING THEME* chapter for details).

1. Navigate to **Dashboard > Posts**. Hover your mouse over the desired post, such as **Hello world!** Additional options will appear.

⬜ **Hello world!**

    Edit | Quick Edit | Trash | View

2. Click on **Quick Edit**. This will reveal page options.

3. In the **Quick Edit** menu, you have the option to adjust certain post properties without opening the full post editor.

4. Select the option **Make this post sticky**.

5. Click **Update** and then view the site to see the changes.

Turn off Allow comments

For an informational site, you may not want readers to comment on posts. In such cases, you can disable the comment form.

1. Go to **Dashboard > Posts**. Hover your mouse over the desired post (e.g., Hello World!). Additional options will appear.

2. Click on **Quick Edit**. You'll see various options.

3. Disable the **Allow Comments** option. This will remove the comment form from the post. Click **Update** to save the changes.

If you want to disable comments for all new posts:

Go to **Dashboard > Settings > Discussion**.

Discussion Settings

Default post settings   ☐ Attempt to notify any blogs linked to from the post

☐ Allow link notifications from other blogs (pingbacks and trackbacks) on new posts

☐ Allow people to submit comments on new posts

Individual posts may override these settings. Changes here will only be applied to new posts.

Under **Default Post Settings**, uncheck all options related to comments. Save the changes. This helps prevent spam.

Protecting pages with a password

While most of your site is accessible to the public, you may want to restrict access to certain parts. Pages or posts can be password protected.

Go to **Dashboard > Pages**.
Hover over the title of the page you want to protect and click **Quick Edit**.

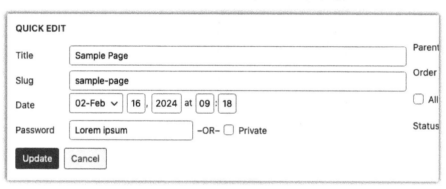

Enter a **password** in the Password field to protect the page.

Alternatively, you can set the page to **Private**, allowing only registered users to view it after logging in (see *Users* chapter). In this case, a password is not required.

Click the **Update** button to save the changes.

MEDIA LIBRARY

You can access the media library from the Media section in your WordPress dashboard. From here, you can upload and organize your media files. Once uploaded, you can easily insert media files into your theme, posts, pages, or widget areas as needed.

We are going to add a file to the library:

1. Go to **Dashboard > Media > Add New Media File**.

2. Drag and drop a file into this window or click **Select Files**.

3. After the file is uploaded, you'll be shown additional information.

4. To manage your media files, go to go to **Dashboard > Media > Library**. From this window, you can view and organize all media files.

5. When you click on an image, you'll see five options: **Edit image**, **View media file**, **Edit more details**, **Download file**, and **Delete permanently**.

Click **Edit more details** to add meta information such as a **Title**, **Alternative Text**, **Caption**, and **Description**.

Then click the **Update** button.

Edit image

To edit an image, click on it and then click the **Edit Image** button.

The editing options include **Crop**, **Scale**, **Rotate** and **Flip**.

You can also adjust the original size in the right column.

After making changes, click the **Apply** button.

Place image

You can place images in a Post or Page. From the block editor, first click on the + icon and then choose **Image**.

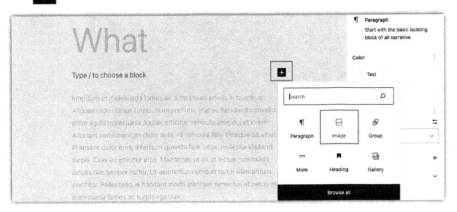

You will see a total overview in a popup window.

1. Select an image and click the **Select** button.

2. Then click on an **alignment** icon. In this case, choose align **left**.

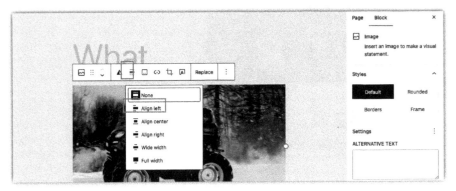

3. Then click the **+** icon again and select a **Paragraph**.

Place text in the paragraph block. The image is now left-aligned relative to the text. Make the image smaller to see the effect.

You can edit an image by clicking on the image. In the right column you'll see a number of settings. If you click on **Options** (3 dots, toolbar) you can *copy*, *duplicate* or *delete* an image.

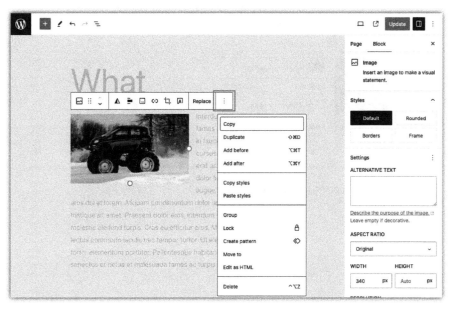

Link image

An image can also be used as a link. Select an image. Then click on the **Link** icon in the block editor. As you can see, it is possible to link to a **URL**, **Media file** (large image) or **Attachment page** (large image in page).

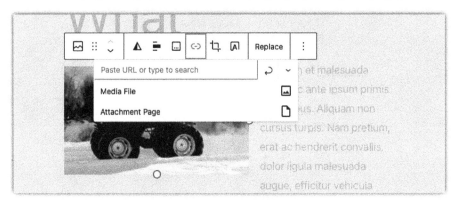

Type or paste a URL into the link field. The **Link Settings > Open in New Tab** button opens the link in a new window. Then click the **Apply** button.

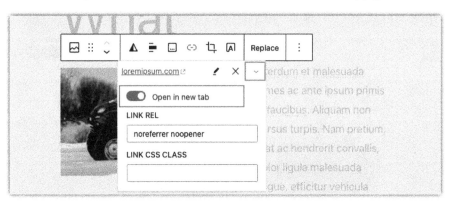

After that, don't forget to **Update** the page.

Media settings

Go to **Dashboard > Settings > Media**.

The values indicate the maximum dimensions in pixels used to add images to the media library.

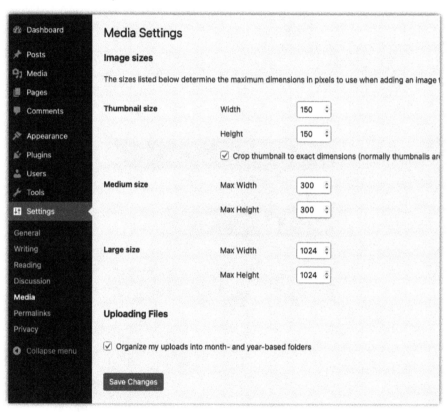

If you want to deviate from this, you can change it.

Then don't forget to click the **Save Changes** button.

MENU

With the Twenty Twenty-One theme, Pages are not automatically included in a Menu, unlike some themes. If you want to have a menu and control its order yourself, you'll need to create one. Follow these steps:

1. Go to
Dashboard > Appearance > Menus.

2. In the **Menu Name** field, give your menu a name, such as *Main Menu*, and then click the **Create Menu** button.

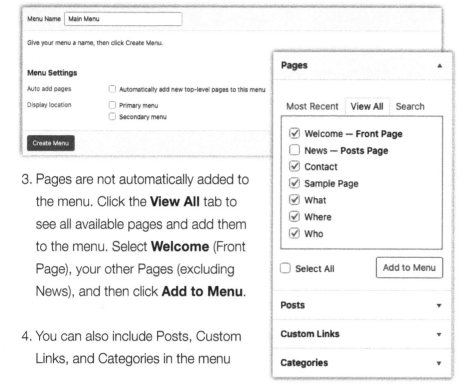

3. Pages are not automatically added to the menu. Click the **View All** tab to see all available pages and add them to the menu. Select **Welcome** (Front Page), your other Pages (excluding News), and then click **Add to Menu**.

4. You can also include Posts, Custom Links, and Categories in the menu

5. Adjust the order of the menu items by dragging them vertically. To create submenus, drag a menu item to the right (e.g., **Who > Sample Page**).

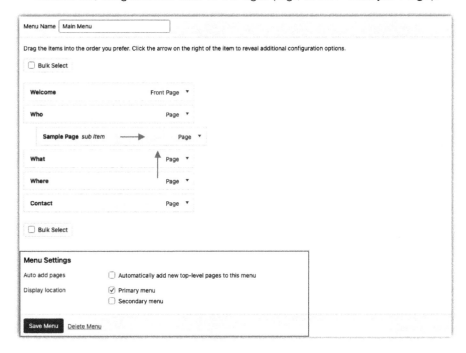

6. In **Menu Settings**, activate **Primary Menu** to display the menu on the website. Different themes may have various locations for menus, each with its own position and style.

7. Once you've customized the menu, click **Save Menu** and preview your site.

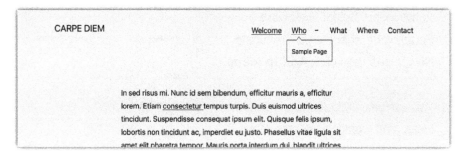

Posts in menu

In the *Customize Home* chapter, it's mentioned that all Posts will be linked to the News Page. Follow these steps to add the News page to the menu:

1. Add the **News** page to the menu.

2. Drag the menu item to the desired location, for example, above Contact.

3. Click **Save Menu** and view the site.

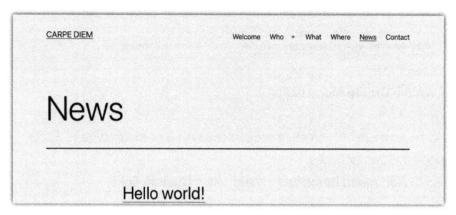

Social links menu

Under **Menu settings > Display location**, you'll find several location names. The number and names of locations may vary by theme, determined
by the theme itself (in this case, Twenty Twenty-One).

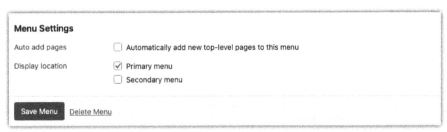

A menu can be included in different areas like the header, footer, left column, etc. If you see a location named **Social Menu**, it's specifically inten-
ded for a menu that includes links to social media pages. In a Social Menu,
social media icons are automatically generated. In the Twenty Twenty-One
theme, you can use the **Secondary menu** location, which is typically displayed in the footer.

Creating a social menu
Go to **create a new menu** and name it **Social Menu**.

Edit Menus | **Manage Locations**

Edit your menu below, or create a new menu. Do not forget to save your changes!

Click the **Create Menu** button.

As an example, let's create a social menu with links to WordPress' *Facebook* and *Twitter* pages.

Go to **Add menu items** section and select **Custom links**.

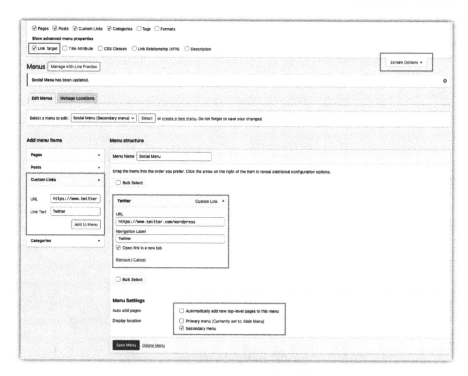

URL : *https://www.facebook.com/wordpress*. **Link text** : **Facebook**.

Then click the **Add to Menu** button. Do the same for Twitter.

URL - *https://www.twitter.com/wordpress*. **Link text** - **Twitter**.

Using the **Screen Options** (located at the top right of the screen), you can set the **Link Target** to *open a link in a new tab*. This option is available after activation and can be set for each menu item individually.

In **Menu settings**, under *Display location*, select **Secondary menu**.

Finally, click the **Save Menu** button and view the site (footer).

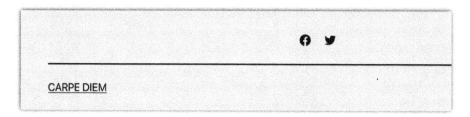

CATEGORIES

In WordPress, you can **categorize** your **posts** to make them easier for visitors to find.

Categories can be displayed in menus or used in sidebars.

1. Go to **Dashboard > Posts > Categories**.

2. Hover over **Uncategorized** and click **Quick Edit**.

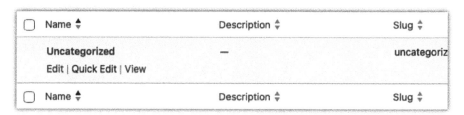

3. Change the name to **Blog Posts** and click **Update Category**.

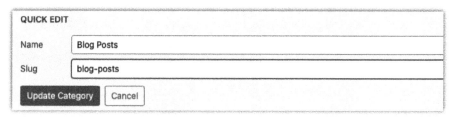

You can also keep the *Uncategorized* category and create new ones as needed. This can be helpful for organizing posts that haven't been categorized yet.

Under **Add New Category** enter the name of the new category.

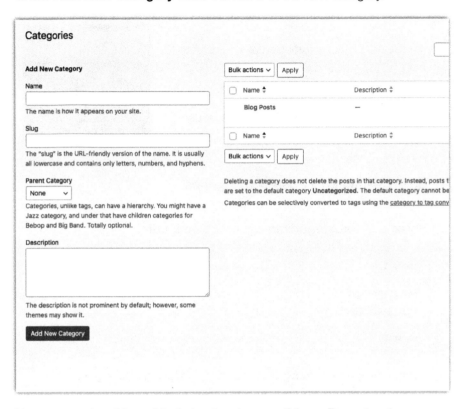

You can create a hierarchical structure by specifying a **Parent category**. Click the **Add New Category** button when finished.

For example, if you're blogging about sports, s*ports* could be a Parent category, with subcategories like *soccer*, *basketball*, and volleyball.

After creating categories, you can assign them to your posts.

Go to **Dashboard > Posts > All Posts**. Select a post.

Change the categorie as needed.

WIDGETS

Widgets are elements that enhance the visual and interactive features of a website. These components include items like a **Search Field**, **Recent Comments**, **Archive**, **Most Recent Posts**, **Categories**, etc.

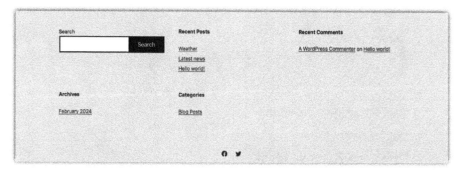

Widgets are commonly found in a theme's **footer** or **sidebar**.

Add widget

1. Go to **Dashboard > Appearance > Widgets**.

2. Scroll down and click on the **+** icon.
   Select a **Calendar** block.

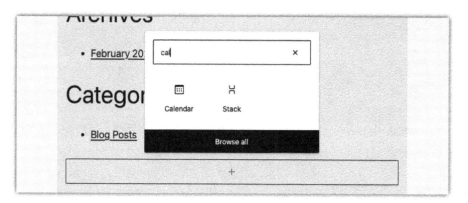

3. **Drag** the block to your desired position, such as at the top.

4. Click **Save**.

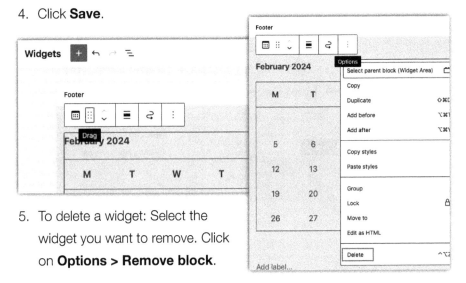

5. To delete a widget: Select the widget you want to remove. Click on **Options > Remove block**.

6. View site.

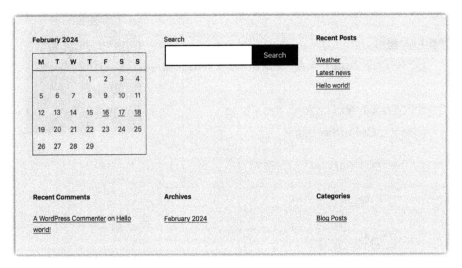

Remember that widgets can vary depending on the theme you're using. If you switch to a different theme, you may need to re-add your widgets.

Content in sidebar or footer

If you wish to add more content to a sidebar, simply click on the **+** icon located at the top left of the screen. All the blocks available in this window can be added to either a sidebar or footer.

To add additional content to a sidebar or footer, follow these steps:

1. Go to **Dashboard > Appearance > Widgets**.
2. Click on the **+** icon.
3. Select a **Heading** block, and add text to it.
4. Select an **Image** block and select an image from the Media Library.
5. Click on both blocks, then hit the **Group icon** (located on the left side of the options bar) and choose **Group**.

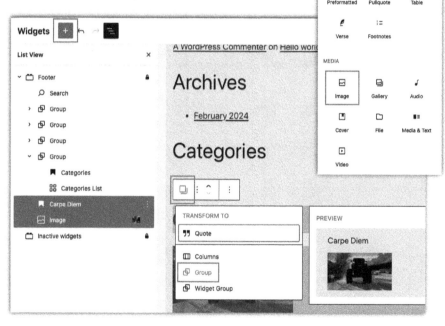

6. Rearrange the order if needed.

7. Save your changes.

8. Preview the site.

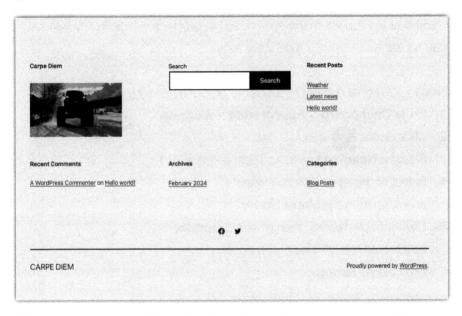

When you group both blocks together, they will appear as a single block (stacked vertically) in the footer. Separate blocks are displayed side by side.

PRACTICAL BLOCKS

As of WordPress version 5.0, it is no longer necessary to install plugins to place columns, tables or buttons, among other things. With the new block editor, users can utilize various elements directly. In this chapter, we'll explore some practical blocks.

Columns

Navigate to a **Page** and click on the ▣ icon at the top left. Choose **DESIGN > Columns**.

Select a variation. It is recommended to use no more than 2 or 3 columns. In a mobile view, columns are displayed below each other.

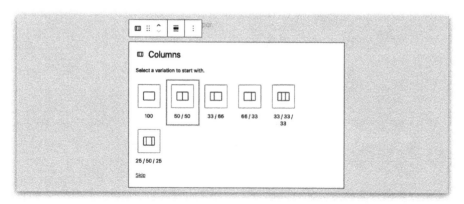

The columns are placed. Inside each column, use the **+** icon to add content blocks like **Paragraph**.

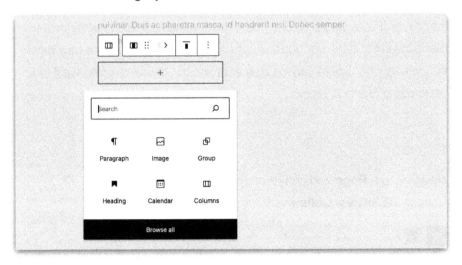

To navigate through nested block elements in a column, use **Document Overview > List View**. This can be found in the upper left corner of the window.

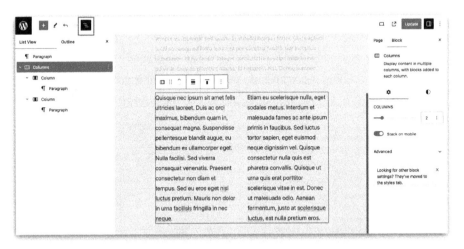

By selecting a block in this list, you can easily modify an element (right).

Tables

Click on the ＋ icon and select **TEXT > Table**.

Specify the desired number of **columns** and **rows**. Then click **Create Table** and place some content in the table.

From the **Table Settings** options activate **Fixed width table cells**.

Buttons

A button gets more attention than a textual link.

Click on the **+** icon and select **DESIGN > Buttons**.

Add **text** in to the **Button**. Click the **link icon** and type or paste a **URL** into the link field. From **Options** (right) you can customize button properties.

Under **Styles**, choose **Fill**. With **Color** you can adjust the Text or Background color. Rounding can be done with **Radius**.

Ensure the link **opens in a new tab** using the Toolbar-Link option.

Then click on the button **Update** or **Publish**.

Gallery

Click on the **+** icon and choose **MEDIA > Gallery**.

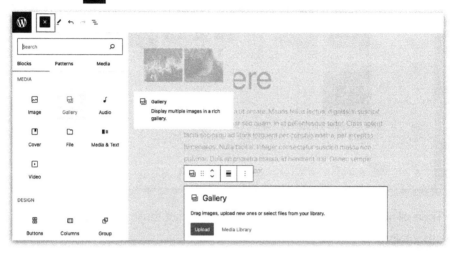

Upload new images or select existing ones from the Media Library.

Click the **Media Library** button and select a number of images.

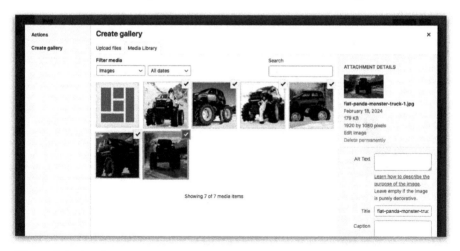

Then click the **Create a new gallery button**.

A new overview screen appears.

Then click **Insert Gallery**. It is possible to adjust the image order, among other things.

Select an **image**. In the **toolbar**, click the **Link icon** and select **Expand on click**.

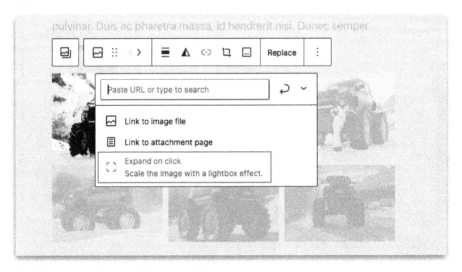

Publish your Post or Page and view the site.

Patterns

Blocks enable you to format pages or posts. Additionally, you have the option to utilize Patterns, which are pre-designed blocks tailored for specific purposes such as a welcome page, blog layout, or contact page, among others.

Patterns come integrated within the active theme. Using Patterns can significantly save time, as they offer ready-made structures that you can easily customize by replacing text or images. You can further enhance the appearance of blocks and patterns by adjusting **settings** in the right column.

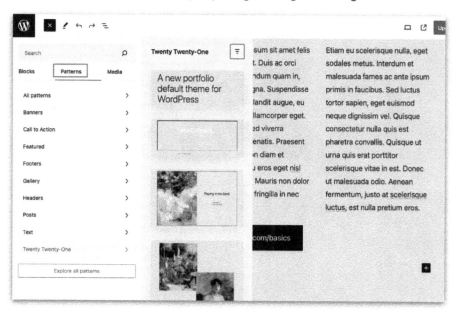

Moreover, WordPress allows you to create **Reusable Blocks**, which serve a similar purpose as patterns. These blocks can be added to your website, providing consistency across different pages. For detailed instructions on creating reusable blocks, refer to the book *WordPress - Gutenberg*.

CUSTOMIZE THEME

Customizing the active theme can be easily done from the Dashboard, with the extent of customization options varying depending on the theme in use.

To access the customization settings, navigate to **Dashboard > Appearance > Themes > Customize**.

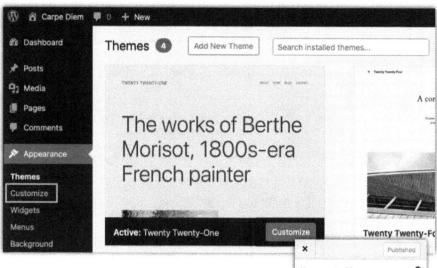

This action opens a new window, where the left column displays a list of customizable items. Each option expands upon clicking, revealing further customization possibilities.

In the case of this theme, customization options include **Site Identity**, **Colors & Dark Mode**, **Background Image**, **Menus**, **Widgets**, **Homepage Settings**, **Excerpt Settings** and **Additional CSS**.

For instance, if you wish to adjust theme colors, you can utilize the **Colors & Dark Mode** option. By clicking on **Select color** next to **Background color**, you can modify the color as desired, with the changes immediately visible in the preview window.

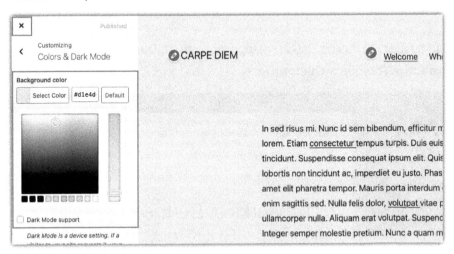

Don't forget to **save** your changes, and then close the customization window by clicking the '**X**' icon at the top left corner.

Place header image

Placing a header image involves selecting an image to be displayed at the top of the theme. While many themes allow this to be done through **Dashboard > Customize > Header**, the Twenty Twenty-One theme utilizes a **Featured Image** instead. To set a Featured Image as the header, follow these steps:

Go to **Dashboard > Pages** and select the homepage **Welcome**. From the **Settings** panel on the right side, click on **Featured Image** and choose a suitable image from your media library. Finally, click the **Update** button to save your changes

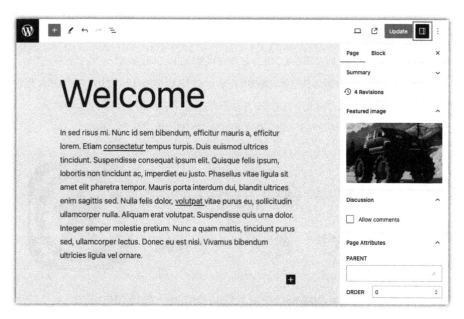

By repeating these steps for each page, you can create a varied header across your site.

Favicon

A favicon (short for favorite icon) is a small icon associated with a website that appears in a browser's address bar and bookmarks. In WordPress, it's recommended that the favicon be square or at least 512 × 512 pixels in size and can be in various web formats such as gif, jpg, or png.

Go to **Dashboard > Appearance > Customize - Site identity**.
Under **Site icon**, click **Select site icon**.

Choose an image from your **media library** and crop it as necessary.

Preview the favicon, and once satisfied, click the **Publish** button to save your changes.

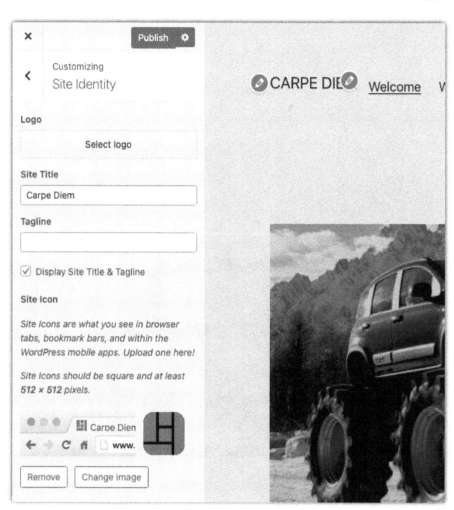

NEW THEME

A WordPress theme is a collection of PHP and CSS files that define the design and functionality of a WordPress site.

Themes allow users to change the site's design without losing content and are also known as templates.

WordPress offers over 11,000 free themes for download, as well as commercial themes ranging from $10 to about $70.

In this chapter, I'll show you how to **download** a theme, **install** and **activate** it.

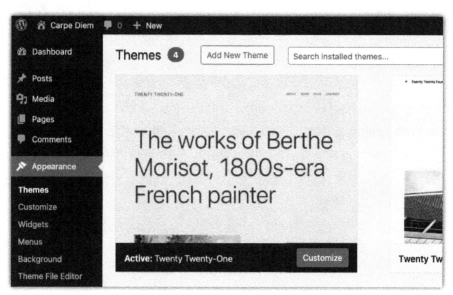

Go to **Dashboard > Appearance > Themes**.
Click the **Add New Theme** button.

Download and install theme

To download and install a theme, you have several options. In the **Add Themes** screen, you'll find categories like **Popular**, **Latest**, **Block Themes**, and **Favorites**.

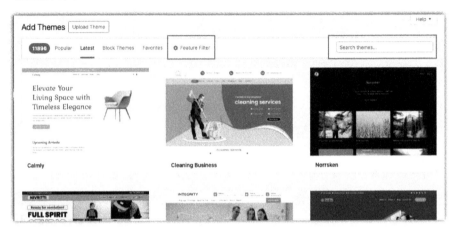

You can also use the **Search Themes** feature or the **Feature Filter** to find a suitable theme.

If you have a theme file downloaded, you can install it by clicking the **Upload Theme** button. The theme file is usually in **Zip** format. For more free themes, you can visit *http://wordpress.org/extend/themes*.

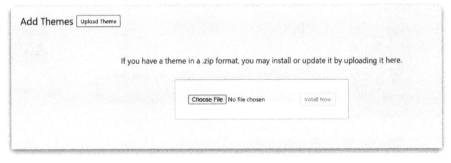

Once you've found a theme you like, click the **Install** button.

For example, let's install the Maxwell theme by ThemeZee. Type **Maxwell** in the **search field**, then click **Search**.

Hover over the theme preview for more information or click **Details & Preview**. Finally, click **Install**.

From **Dashboard > Appearance > Themes** you can see the number of installed themes. **Activate** allows you to change themes.

If you notice the menu disappearing after changing the theme, you can adjust it in **Dashboard > Appearance > Menus**.

In some cases, certain features like the **Social Menu** might require a paid version of the theme. To include social media icons, you can use Widgets or Plugins.

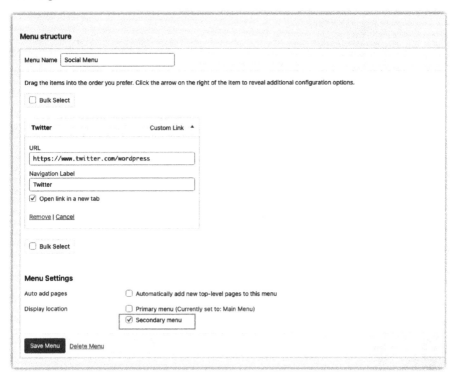

After making changes, remember to specify the **Display location** in Menu settings and click **Save Menu**.

Customize Theme

Customizing a theme using the **Theme Customizer** varies depending on the theme. Let's explore the options available in the Maxwell theme.

Go to **Dashboard > Appearance > Themes > Customize**.

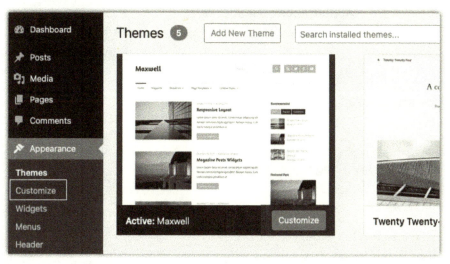

On the left column, you'll see the customization options available.

In the Maxwell theme, you can customize **Site Identity**, **Header Image**, **Background**, **Menus**, **Widgets**, **Homepage Settings**, **Theme Options** and **Additional CSS**.

For instance, to change the theme color, you can use **Background > Background color**.

Place header

Adding a header to the *Maxwell* theme is different from the default *Twenty Twenty-One* theme.

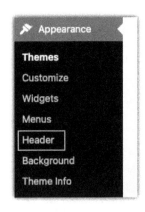

To add a header to the theme go to:
Dashboard > Appearance > Header or
Dashboard > Customize - Header image

Find a suitable header image with dimensions around **1200 x 400 pixels** in JPG format.

Click **Add New Image**, select the file, then **upload** it.

If the image is too large, you may need to crop it. Alternatively, you can skip cropping.

Once uploaded, click **Publish** to save your changes. Preview your site to see the new header.

The header will be displayed on every page and post. If you want different headers for each page or post, you may need to use a plugin.

You can find more details about this in the *Custom Headers* chapter.

Carpe Diem

Welcome   Who ⌄   What   Where   News   Contact

February 16, 2024 • Blog Posts

Hello world!

Welcome to WordPress. This is your first post. Edit or delete it, then start writing!

Continue reading »

February 18, 2024 • Blog Posts

Weather

Nunc pulvinar, enim a faucibus semper, orci augue rutrum metus, a tempor mauris nunc et ligula. Cras dapibus non nunc

Continue reading »

Carpe Diem

Search

BLOCK THEME

The **Twenty Twenty-Two** theme is the first default WordPress block theme. It enables easy visual customization, allowing you to edit or add blocks
such as titles, logos, and menus. You can also adjust the structure of your
homepage, **posts**, or **pages**, along with changing the default footer text
and tweaking styles like color, size, and font.

Customizing a block theme is done using the same editor as for pages or
posts. WordPress calls this **Full Site Editing**, offering a comprehensive site
editor and builder experience. To get started, create a **new WordPress
website** with **Local** (refer to the chapter on *Installing WordPress*).

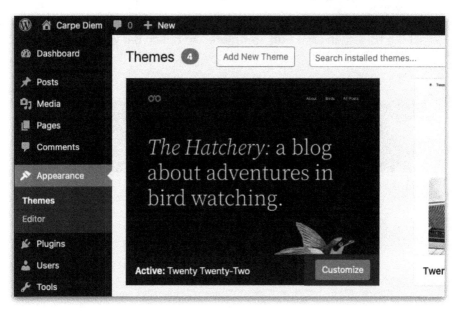

Go to **Dashboard > Appearance** and **install** and **activate** the **Twenty
Twenty-Two** theme. WordPress wants to show in this version how easy it
is to work with block themes.

Go to **Appearance > Editor**. The Site Editor appear. In the left column you'll see a number of options: **Navigation**, **Styles**, **Pages**, **Templates** and **Patterns**. On the right you'll see the homepage with the latest posts.

Select the **title**, then click **Edit Template**. An option bar will appear above the block.

Using the **Settings** icon (top right), you'll find additional **block options** in a right-hand column. With **Block Settings** (column icon) and **Styles** (crescent icon), you can further customize the block.

The **WordPress** icon (top left) will take you back to the Site Editor.

Navigate to **Appearance > Editor - Templates**. Templates are comprised of **Template parts** and **blocks**, collectively forming a page. A template part could be a **Header**, **Sidebar**, or **Footer**, for instance. A template typically consists of multiple parts.

The name of a **Template** indicates its purpose. For example, the Template **Single Posts** is displayed when a visitor clicks on a post from the homepage, showing the entire post. The number of templates may vary depending on the theme.

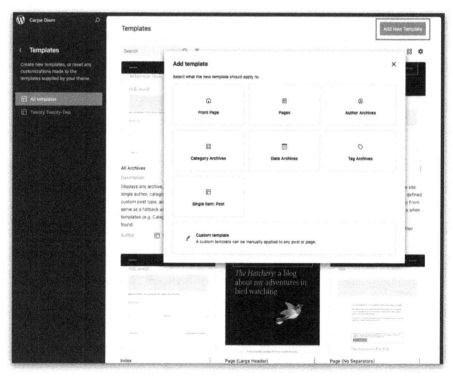

You can create new templates by clicking the button **Add New Template**.

Select **Single Posts** and click on a **block** to edit it.

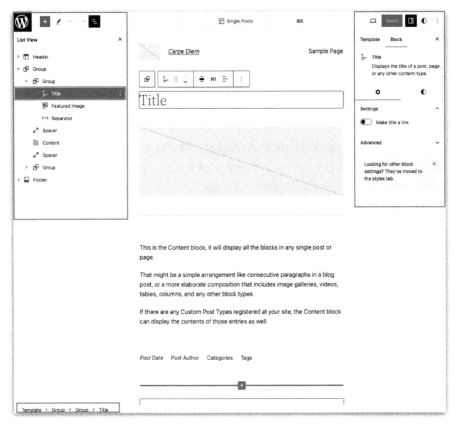

The structure of a template consists of **template parts** and **theme blocks**. By selecting a template component or block, you can see its function. You can do this either by using **List View** or the **breadcrumb trail**. Adjust block properties using the **block options** and **settings** in the right column.

You can add template parts and theme blocks using the block inserter, represented by the ➕ icon at the top left.

Go to **Appearance > Editor > Patterns**. Alongside theme Patterns (layouts), you'll also find a list of TEMPLATE PARTS. Click on a Part to edit it.

The name indicates the type it represents.

With **Add New Pattern > Add New Template Part** you can create template parts.

The benefit of working with a **Template Part** is that it enables you to focus on the layout without being overwhelmed by the entire page structure.

Edit Homepage, Template and Template Parts

With the Site Editor, you can add or change designs easily. Changes take effect immediately when you save. A modified template appears in the template overview. To restore a modified template, go to **Templates > All Templates**. Then, go to **Actions** (three dots) and select **Reset**.

To illustrate, let's proceed to edit a template.

Navigate to **Editor > Templates** and select the **Single Posts** template.

Our objective is to substitute the Header and Footer with a Pattern. Additionally, we'll adjust the Meta information blocks, including Date, Author, and Category, positioned directly below the Title.

Header and Footer customization:

1. Navigate to **List View** and select the **Group** within the **Header**.
2. Click on the ➕ icon and opt for **Patterns**.
3. Select the **Headers** category.
4. Choose **Text-only header with tagline and black background**.
5. **Delete** the **old Group**.
6. Adjust Text and Link color to white.

Repeat the same process for the **footer**, selecting **Dark footer with title and citation**.

Then, move the *Meta information* directly below the **Title** by **selecting** and **dragging** the Meta information **row** under the **Title**.

Utilize the **List View** tool for assistance. Next, adjust the width to **Wide Width**. **Save** your changes and preview a post.

For further insights into layouts, full site editing, and block themes, refer to the book **WordPress Gutenberg** and **WordPress Block Themes**.

Note: **Activate** the **Twenty Twenty-One** theme as you'll need it for the next chapter, or go to your previous WordPress site.

EDIT FOOTER

The footer is located at the bottom of a WordPress theme. In the **Twenty Twenty-One** theme, you'll find the *site title* and the text *Proudly powered by WordPress* in the footer.

You can customize the footer "under the hood".

1. **Activate** the **Twenty Twenty-One** theme.
2. Go to **Dashboard > Appearance > Theme File Editor**.
   A popup window appears. Click on the **I understand** button. After that, you'll be presented with *Twenty Twenty-One* PHP theme files.

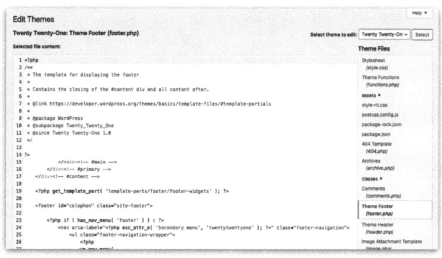

In the **right-hand column** you can see all the **Twenty Twenty-One** theme files.

3. Click on **Theme footer** (footer.php) in the right column. **Tip**: Make a backup of the code first. Copy the code and paste it into a text file. In the window, you may edit the file.

```
63              <div class="powered-by">
64                  <?php
65                  printf(
66                      /* translators: %s: WordPress. */
67                      esc_html__( 'Proudly powered by %s.', 'tw
68                      '<a href="' . esc_url( __( 'https://wordp
69                  );
70                  ?>
71              </div><!-- .powered-by -->
72
73          </div><!-- .site-info -->
74      </footer><!-- #colophon -->
75
```

4. Delete the script between the tags below
   <?php and **?>**, lines 65 to 69.

5. Place new information between these two tags:
   <?php

   ```
   print "Carpe Diem - "; echo date('D, d, M, Y');
   ```

   ?>

```
62
63              <div class="powered-by">
64                  <?php
65                  print "Carpe Diem - "; echo date('D, d, M, Y');
66                  ?>
67              </div><!-- .powered-by -->
68
```

6. The script after "Carpe Diem - " generates the current date.
   ('D, d, M, Y') = day, digit, month and year. If desired,
   remove one of the letters to adjust the date.
   Tip: Note the quotation marks. "wrong" - "right".

7. Click the **Update File** button and view the site.

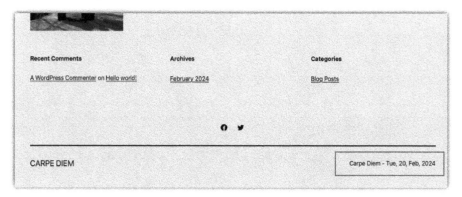

This exercise shows you where to go to modify a theme file. Unfortunately, theme updates will overwrite any modifications made to the footer.

If you want to make a permanent change then a **Child Theme** of the original theme must be created. This is a kind of copy of the original theme.

If you are using a Block theme (see chapter *BLOCK THEME*), then you can use the Site Editor. It is then no longer necessary to modify a PHP file for this purpose.

If you like modifying code "under the hood" or want to know how a Child Theme is created, check out the book **WordPress - Advanced**.

USERS

In WordPress, different users can have access to managing a website. Giving users different permissions gives them full or limited access.

Adding users:

1. Go to **Dashboard > Users > Add New User**.

   Add a new user.

   Make sure you have completed the required fields.

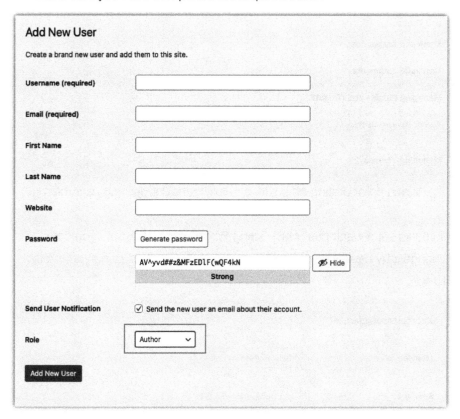

2. Assign a **Role** (permissions) to the new user before adding them.

Overview of different roles:

	Subscriber	Contributor	Author	Editor	Administrator
Read posts	●	●	●	●	●
Commenting on Posts	●	●	●	●	●
Change or delete posts		●	●	●	●
Publish posts			●	●	●
Upload and manage media files			●	●	●
Edit, delete or publish Posts and Pages				●	●
Managing Categories				●	●
Managing comments				●	●
Managing Plugins and Widgets					●
Add or remove users					●
Managing Themes					●

Tip: When collaborating on a site, carefully consider defining user roles.

If you've set a weak password during WordPress installation, you can change it by navigating to **Dashboard > Users** and selecting your profile to edit.

Account Management

New Password   Set New Password

Sessions   Log Out Everywhere Else

Did you lose your phone or leave your account logged in at a public comp

WORDPRESS PLUGINS

Building additional functionality into WordPress is accomplished through plugins, among other methods. These can be thought of as additional programs within the system. If you find something missing in WordPress, such as a mail form, a gallery, or search engine optimization, there's likely a plugin available to fulfill that need.

While there are numerous plugins available, it is important to proceed wisely. Don't overload your site with plugins. Use them only when necessary; too many plugins can cause conflicts and slow down your site. Moreover, the risk of your site being compromised through a plugin increases. Therefore, it is advisable to thoroughly research a plugin before installing it.

Download Plugin

To download a plugin, visit the WordPress plugin repository at:

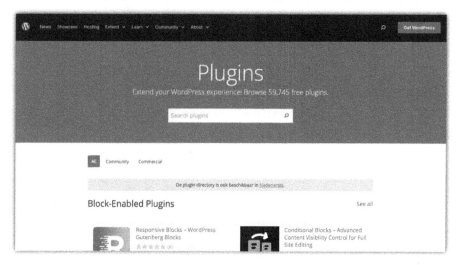

https://wordpress.org/plugins.

The right plugin

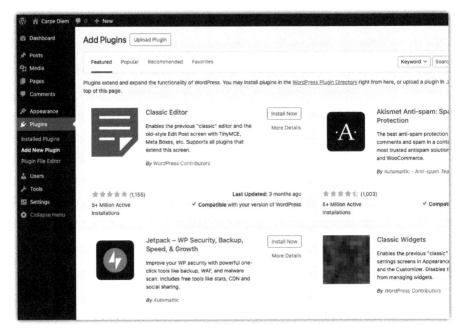

When selecting a plugin, carefully review its information and ask the following questions:

- ▸ Has the plugin received positive ratings?
- ▸ Is the plugin user-friendly for both administrators and visitors?
- ▸ Does the plugin perform as advertised?
- ▸ Is the plugin compatible with the current version of WordPress?
- ▸ How many active installations does the plugin have?
- ▸ Has the site's performance been affected after activating the plugin?

If a plugin fails to meet expectations, remove it promptly and search for an alternative.

Install Plugin

Go to **Dashboard > Plugins > Add New Plugin**.

In the search field, type **Contact Form 7**.
Once the plugin appears, click on **More Details**
for additional information.

Then, click the **Install Now** button, followed by **Activate**.

To view installed plugins, go to **Dashboard > Plugins**.

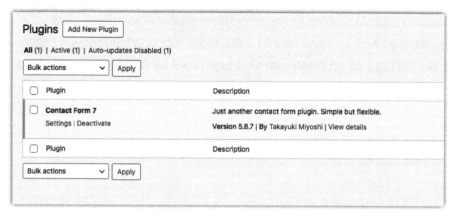

To configure the plugin, visit **Dashboard > Contact**. This section will be added to your Dashboard, providing information on customization and usage.

The plugin can also be accessed in the Block editor.

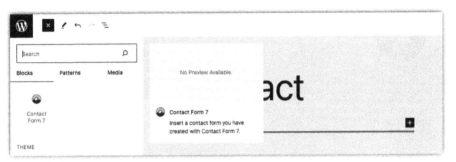

Navigate to a Page, click on the + icon, select **Widgets > Contact Form 7**. Choose *Contact Form 1* and click **Save** or **Update**.

Additionally, plugins can be searched for and downloaded from *word-press.org/plugins*. Remember to install the downloaded plugin as a compressed (.zip) file via **Dashboard > Plugins > Add New Plugin > Upload Plugin**.

To remove a plugin, go to **Dashboard > Plugins > Installed Plugins**. Deactivate a plugin before uninstalling it.

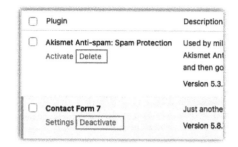

Contact Form 7 is a practical plugin, but if you require more form fields, consider exploring other options. Deactivate and remove Contact Form 7 in preparation for creating a more extensive form in the next chapter.

Favorite plugins

If there are certain plugins you frequently use, mark them as **favorites** on *WordPress.org*. This will allow you to quickly locate them via **Dashboard > Plugins > New Plugin - Favorites**.

Ensure you have an account on WordPress.org to access this feature: *http://wordpress.org/support/register.php*.

Stay tuned for the next chapter, where I'll introduce some useful plugins.

Akismet

WordPress comes with the Akismet plugin by default. If you enable the feature allowing visitors to comment on posts, this plugin safeguards your site against spam comments. To utilize Akismet, activate the plugin and obtain an API key, which can be requested for free.

To request an API key, visit: *https://akismet.com/plans*.
Choose **Get Personal** and fill in the required details on the next page.
Adjust the **contribution slider** to **zero** and click **Continue**.

Your API key will be sent to you via email.

Activating Akismet and Entering the API Key:
Go to **Dashboard > Plugins** and **Install** and **Activate** the Akismet plugin. Configure your Akismet account by entering the **API** key in the provided window. Click the **Connect** button to finalize the setup process.

Under construction

This plugin enables you to shield your website from public view, allowing only logged-in users to access it. The choice of an Under Construction plugin should consider its rating, usability, and number of downloads.

As an example, let's try the **LightStart - Maintenance Mode** plugin.

Install

1. Go to **Dashboard > Plugins > Add New Plugin**.
2. In the search field, type *LightStart - Maintenance Mode*.
3. **Install** and **activate** the plugin.

After activating the plugin, you can select a free template and configure its settings.

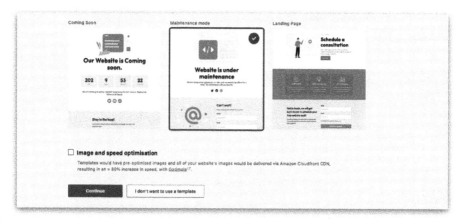

Usage

After choosing a template, you'll be shown the settings.

This can be found under **Dashboard > LightStart**.

1. At **General** tab, select **Status - Activated/Deactivated**.

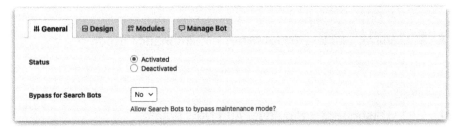

2. Under tab **Design**, you can edit the page or choose another template.

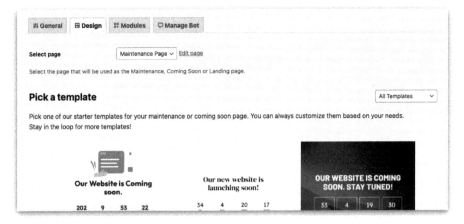

3. Click on the **Modules** tab. You'll see additional settings for extending the plugin.

4. Click the **Manage Bot** tab. This sets up call steps to request email addresses. Choose **Status - Activated**.

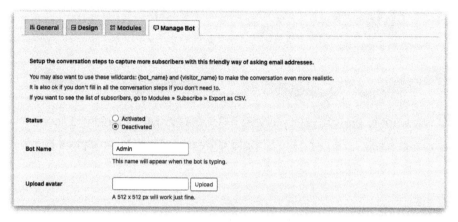

Then click the **Save Settings** button.

5. View your site in a **different browser**.

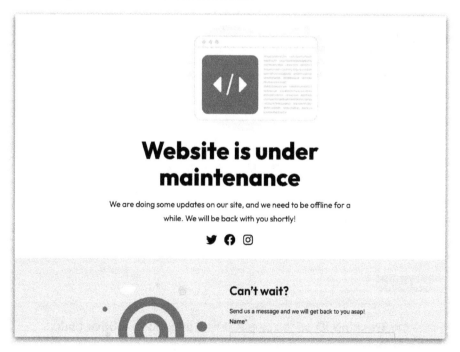

Google analytics

If you want to provide your site with a Google Analytics Tracking ID code, you can easily do so with the **Simple Universal Google Analytics** plugin.

Install

1. Go to **Dashboard > Plugins > Add New Plugin**.
2. In the search field, type *Simple Universal Google Analytics*.
3. **Install** and **activate** the plugin.

Usage

Go to **Dashboard > Settings > Google Analytics**.

Place the **Tracking ID** code in the text field and click the **Save** button.

Form

For a simple form, you can use *Contact Form 7*. However, if you require additional fields, consider using the **wpforms** plugin.

Install

Go to **Dashboard > Plugins > Add New Plugin**.
In the search field, type: *wpforms*. **Install** and **activate** the plugin.

**Contact Form by WPForms – Drag & Drop
Form Builder for WordPress**

The best WordPress contact form plugin. Drag & Drop
online form builder to create beautiful contact forms,
payment forms, & other custom forms ...

Install Now

More Details

Use

Go to **Dashboard > WPForms > Add New**.

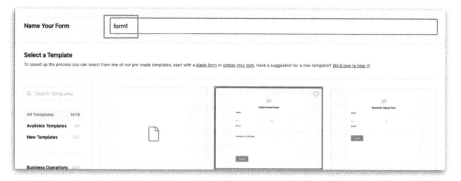

Enter the Form name as **form1** and select **Simple contact form**.

After creating the form, add additional fields as needed.

Click on the **Checkboxes** button.

Select the **checkboxes** from the form.

Customize the **Label** (title) and **Choices**. In this case, the title is *Favorite Color* and the choices are *Red*, *Yellow* and *Blue*. You can rearrange the choice fields by picking them up and dragging them to the desired position. Go to the top right and click the **Save** button, then the **cross** (top right).

Go to **Dashboard > Pages - Contact** and click on the [+] icon.

Go to **Blocks > WIDGETS > WPForms** and select **form1**.

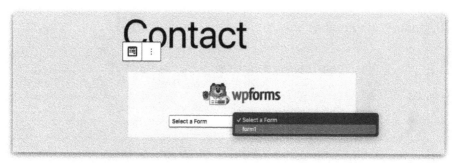

Click the **Save** or **Update** button and View your page.

Form messages not arriving

Form messages not arriving in WordPress can be a common issue, often due to server settings. To ensure reliable delivery of emails from your website, you can use the **WP Mail SMTP** plugin. This plugin allows you to send emails via the SMTP protocol, reducing the likelihood of messages being marked as spam.

Install

1. Go to **Dashboard > Plugins > Add New Plugin**.
2. In the search field, type *WP Mail SMTP*.
3. **Install** and **activate** the plugin.

WP Mail SMTP by WPForms – The Most Popular SMTP and Email Log Plugin

Make email delivery easy for WordPress. Connect with SMTP, Gmail, Outlook, SendGrid, Mailgun, SES, Zoho, + more. Rated #1 WordPress SMTP Email plugin.

By WP Mail SMTP

Install Now

More Details

Usage

Go to **Dashboard > WP Mail SMTP**.

General	Email Log	Alerts	Additional Connections	Smart Routing	Email Controls	Misc

In the **General** tab, choose a Mailer option. Use the email address and SMTP data provided by your web host.

1. **E-mail**: e-mail address and sender name.

2. **Mailer**: select *Other SMTP service*.

3. **Other SMTP**: e.g. *smtp.-domainname.com*.

   Encryption - None.

   Authentication - ON.

   SMPT user name and **password**.

Click on **Save Settings** to apply the changes.

By using WP Mail SMTP, you can ensure that form messages are reliably delivered to your visitors without being marked as spam.

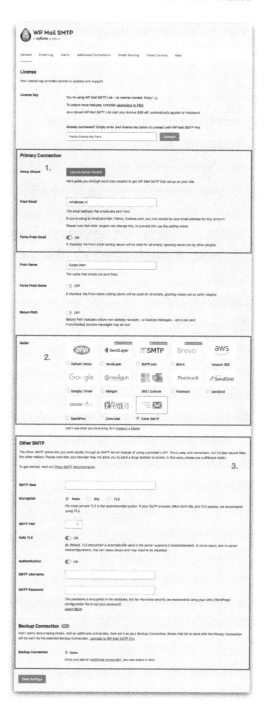

Extend media management

The default WordPress Media Library lacks a folder structure, displaying all media files in a single window and allowing selection only by file type. However, with the **FileBird** plugin, you can organize files into folders.

FileBird is available as a Freemium plugin, meaning a free (Lite) version is available, but with limited features. The Lite version permits the creation of up to 10 folders.

Install

1. Go to **Dashboard > Plugins > Add New Plugin**.
2. In the search field, type *FileBird*.
3. **Install** and **activate** the plugin.

FileBird – WordPress Media Library Folders & File Manager

Organize thousands of WordPress media files in folders / categories with ease.

By *Ninja Team*

Install Now

More Details

Usage

Go to **Dashboard > Media > Library**.

Click the **+ New Folder** button to create a folder.

Drag and **drop** images into the newly created folder.

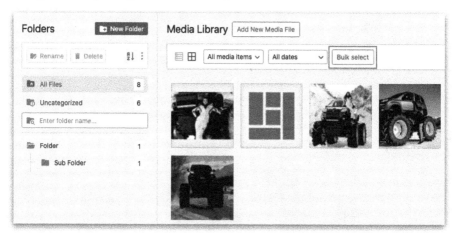

Utilize the **Bulk Select** button to move multiple images into a folder simultaneously.

Creating **subfolders** is straightforward: create a new folder and drag it into an existing folder. To remove a file from a folder, select the folder and drag the file to another folder or to **No Category**.

The Lite version of FileBird allows for the creation of 10 folders. If you require more folders, you'll need to upgrade to the Pro version, available for $39.

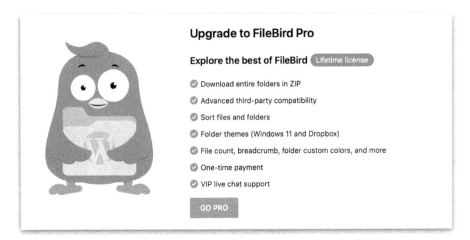

For more information and to upgrade, visit:

ninjateam.org/wordpress-media-library-folders.

Gallery extension

If you have created a standard WordPress gallery, you can enhance its functionality by using the **Simple Lightbox** plugin, which adds a Lightbox effect to your gallery. This effect allows users to click on an image within the gallery to view an enlarged version. Additionally, the gallery functions as a carousel slider.

Install

1. Go to **Dashboard > Plugins > Add New Plugin**.
2. In the search field, type *Simple Lightbox.*
3. **Install** and **Activate** this plugin.

To activate the Lightbox effect in a gallery, navigate to a page containing a Gallery block (refer to the *Gallery* chapter). Simple Lightbox also works with images, buttons, and links, providing an enhanced viewing experience for various types of media.

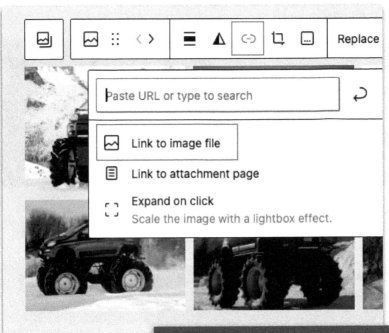

Select the **Gallery** block, in the **Toolbar**, ensure that each image within the gallery **links to** a **image file**.

After making these adjustments, remember to click the **Update** button and then view your site to see the changes.

For further settings go to **Dashboard > Appearance > Lightbox**.

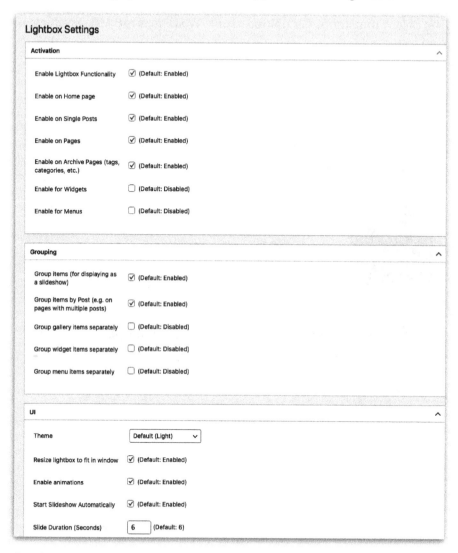

Scroll to the bottom of the page, where you can translate **Labels** as needed. Once done, don't forget to click the **Save Changes** button to apply your settings.

Increase upload size

The default **maximum file upload size** in WordPress is 8 MB, which may not be sufficient for larger files like movies. However, you can increase this limit with the help of a plugin.

Install

1. Go to **Dashboard > Plugins > Add New Plugin**.
2. In the search field, type Increase *Maximum Upload File Size* (Imagify).
3. **Install** and **activate** the plugin.

Increase Maximum Upload File Size

Increase maximum upload file size limit to any value. Increase upload limit - upload large files.

By Imagify

Install Now

More Details

Usage

Go to **Dashboard > Settings > Increase Maximum Upload File Size**. Select your desired value, for example, **64MB**.

General settings   More optimization   About us

Important: if you want to upload files larger than 300MB (which is the limit set by your hosting provider) you have to contact your hosting provider. It's **NOT POSSIBLE** to increase that hosting defined upload limit from a plugin.

Maximum upload file size, set by your hosting provider: 300MB
Maximum upload file size, set by WordPress: 64MB

Choose Maximum Upload File Size   64MB ∨

Click the **Save Changes** button and verify the updated upload size.

Drop files to upload

or

Select Files

Maximum upload file size: 64 MB.

Custom sidebars

Users often have questions about using different sidebars. The *Custom Sidebars* plugin addresses this need by allowing you to create multiple sidebars with different sets of widgets.

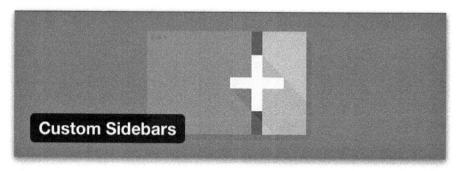

Note: The plugin is incompatible with the Gutenberg Widget Block Editor. Therefore, it's advisable to install the **Classic Widgets** plugin (from WordPress Contributors) before using **Custom Sidebars**.

> 🔥 **IMPORTANT** 🔥
>
> Custom Sidebars plugin is NOT compatible with the new widgets edit screen (powered by Gutenberg). Install the official Classic Widgets plugin if you want to continue using it.

Install

Go to **Dashboard > Plugins > Add New Plugin**. In the search field, type *Custom Sidebars*. **Install** and **activate** the plugin. Then **Install** and **activate** the plugin.

Custom Sidebars – Dynamic Sidebar Widget Area Manager

More Details

Flexible sidebars for custom widget configurations on any page or post. Create custom sidebars with ease!

By WebFactory Ltd

Usage

Go to **Dashboard > Appearance > Widgets**.

Click on **+ Create a new sidebar**.

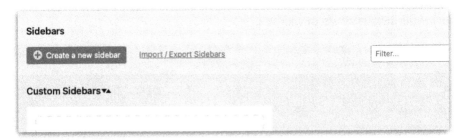

Provide a **Name** and **Description** for the new sidebar.

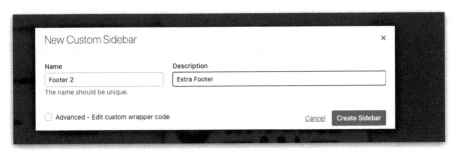

Then click the **Create Sidebar** button.

Add desired widgets to the newly created sidebar, such as **Footer 2**.

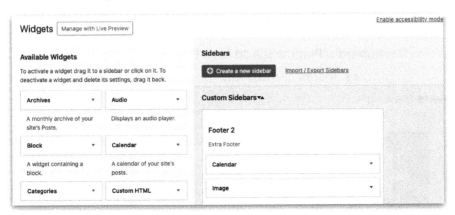

No need to save the changes.

Proceed to **Dashboard > Pages** and select a page to associate with the new sidebar. In the **Sidebars** section, choose **Footer 2**. Click the **Update** button to save the changes.

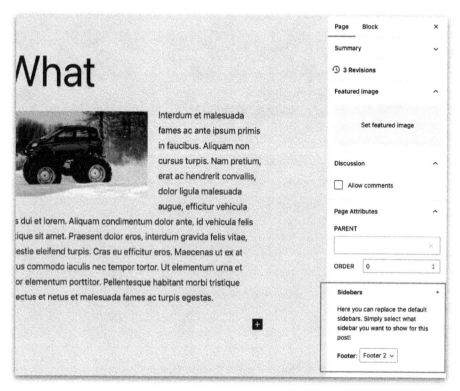

Make sure the page is included in the menu. View the site and click on the corresponding menu item to see the new sidebar in action.

Custom headers

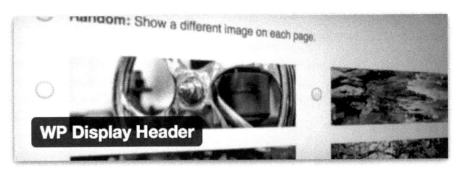

You can enhance your website further by incorporating different header images, provided your theme supports header customization. To utilize this feature, activate the **Maxwell** theme. The **WP Display Header** plugin works similarly to the *Custom Sidebars plugin*.

From a Page or Post, you can specify the corresponding header. When the page is loaded, the header will change accordingly. However, please note that the plugin is not suitable for block themes.

Install

1. Go to **Dashboard > Plugins > Add New Plugin**.
2. In the search field, type *WP Display Header*.
3. **Install** and **activate** the plugin.

WP Display Header

Select a specific header or random header image for each content item or archive page.

By Konstantin Obenland

Install Now

More Details

Important: Ensure that you have activated a classic theme that supports custom headers.

Import new headers

Go to **Dashboard > Media**. Click on **Add New Media File**.

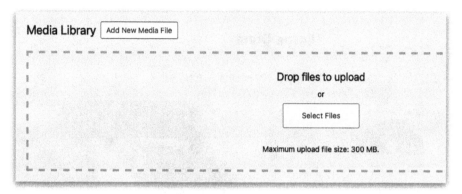

Import several header images.

Tip: Make sure all header images are the same height.

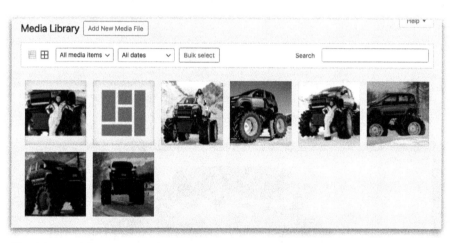

The Maxwell theme specifies that a header should be 1200 × 400 pixels.
After uploading, you can still crop an image to ensure a perfect fit.

Go to **Dashboard > Appearance > Header**.

Click on **Add New Images** and select your new header image.

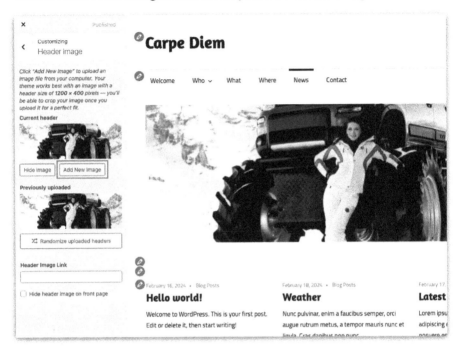

If necessary, you can crop the header image.

In that case, click the **Select and crop** button. The newly added headers will appear in the left column. Additionally, you have the option to set a new image as the default header by selecting it. You can also choose to have your headers displayed randomly. Once you're satisfied with your selection, click the **Publish** button.

Apply

Go to **Dashboard > Pages**. Click on the desired page. In the **Header** section at the bottom of the page, select the corresponding header.

Then click the **Update** button. If the page is included in the menu, the new header will be displayed when a visitor clicks on it.

BACKUP

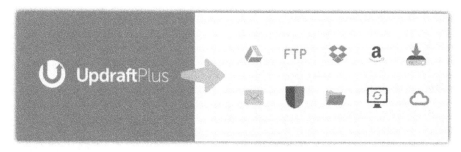

While web hosts typically offer regular website backups, if you prefer not to rely solely on this, you can utilize the **UpdraftPlus WordPress Backup** Plugin. With this plugin, you can easily and swiftly create backups on your own terms, and conveniently revert to previous saved versions if needed.

Using the plugin's settings, you have the flexibility to choose where to store your backups, whether it's in the cloud or on your computer.

Install

1. Go to **Dashboard > Plugins > Add New Plugin**.
2. In the search field, enter *UpdraftPlus WordPress Backup*.
3. **Install** and **activate** the plugin.

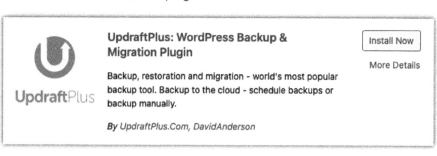

Usage

Go to **Dashboard > UpdraftPlus**.

To perform a manual backup, click the **Backup Now** button.

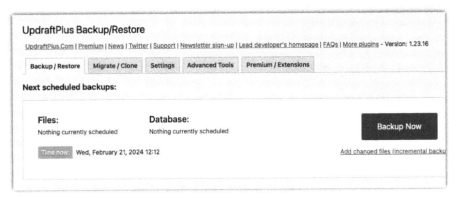

A pop-up window will appear indicating that a backup of your database and WordPress files is in progress. You can opt to set manual deletion for this backup.

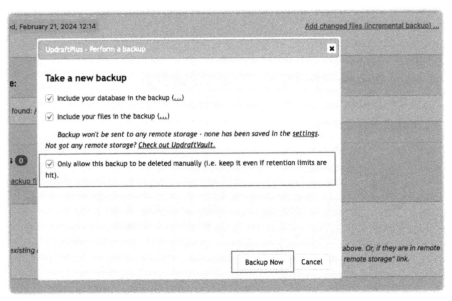

Click the **Back Up Now** button to initiate the backup process.

Your backup is now saved. Should you need to restore to a previous version, simply use the **Restore** button.

If you prefer to save your backup locally or in the cloud, navigate to the **Settings** tab. Here, you can specify the location for your next backup.

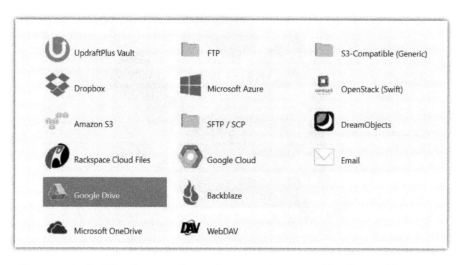

Please note that the free version only supports manual backups. For automatic backups and additional features, you can consider upgrading to the Premium version. For more information, visit: *https://updraftplus.com*.

SECURE SITE

WordPress is generally a secure and extensively tested platform. However, occasional hacking incidents may occur, often caused by security issues at web hosts, vulnerabilities in plugins, weak login credentials or outdated WordPress versions.

To enhance your site's security, you can utilize **Solid Security**, a plugin designed to fix potential security holes, obstruct automated attacks, and fortify the login process.

Install

1. Go to **Dashboard > Plugins > Add New Plugin**.
2. Search for *Solid Security* in the search field.
3. **Install** and **activate** the plugin.

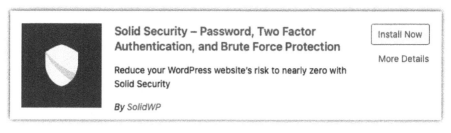

Go to **Dashboard > Security**. Follow the configuration process to secure your site. Choose the options that best suit your site's needs.

Answer a few questions to enable key security features tailored for your site. Once configured, you'll see an overview of your security settings.

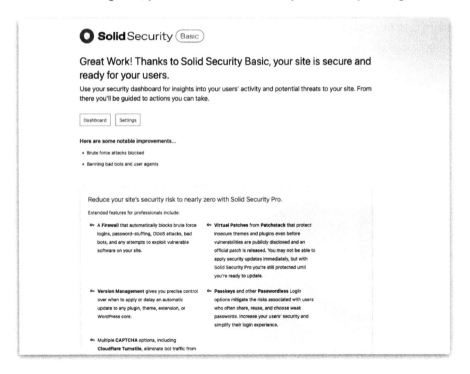

Go to **Dashboard > Security > Settings** to explore additional features.

Under **Features > Firewall**, enable Network Brute Force Protection.

Utilize the **Help** button for further explanations on using security features.

To activate specific functions, click the **Enable** button and configure the options as needed.

If you require advanced security features, consider upgrading to the Pro version of the plugin. The Pro version offers comprehensive security measures and support. Pricing starts at $99.

For more information, visit: *https://solidwp.com/security*.

MOVING A LOCAL SITE TO THE INTERNET

If you've built a WordPress site on a local web server like LOCAL or MAMP and now want to take it online, the **All-in-One WP Migration** plugin can help you seamlessly move your website.

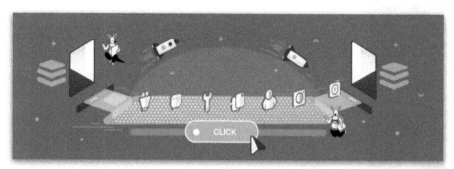

In this guide, we'll walk through **exporting** a local WordPress site and then **importing** it to an online WordPress site. This method works in reverse as well. It's important to note that the file used for exporting the website also serves as a backup of the site.

Install Plugin

1. Go to **Dashboard > Plugins > Add New Plugin**.
2. Search for **All-in-One WP Migration** in the search field.
3. **Install** and **activate** the plugin.

All-in-One WP Migration   Install Now

Move, transfer, copy, migrate, and backup a site with 1-   More Details
click. Quick, easy, and reliable.

By ServMask

Exporting the Site

1. Go to **Dashboard > All-in-One WP Migration**.

   Click on the **Export To** button and choose the **File** option.

2. Wait while the system scans the site.

3. Once scanned, click the green **DOWNLOAD** button.

4. The export file with the **.wpress** extension will be available in your Downloads folder.

Importing the site

1. Access your web hosting platform (e.g., *IONOS*) and install a new WordPress site using the Apps installer.

2. Install and activate the **All-in-One WP Migration** plugin on the new WordPress site.

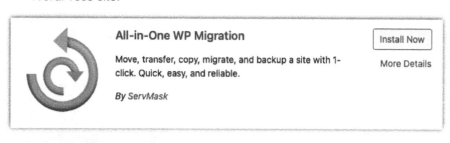

3. Go to **Dashboard > All-in-One WP Migration > Import**.
4. Click on **IMPORT FROM** and select the **File** option.
   Choose the **.wpress** file or drag and drop it into the upload box.

> Tip: If your site is too large to import directly, you can also install the **All-in-One WP Migration Import** plugin. You can download this additional plugin from: *https://import.wp-migration.com*.

5. The installation process is ongoing.

6. Once imported, you'll see a message. Click **Proceed** to continue.

7. Your site (data) has been imported successfully!

8. Follow any additional instructions provided.

9. **Note!** Use the login credentials from your imported site.

10. Go to **Dashboard > Settings > Permalinks**. Choose the Post Name setting.

11. Click on the **Save Changes** button.

Congratulations! Your WordPress site has been successfully imported.

Remember to regularly export a **.wpress** file after making changes or updates to serve as a backup of your site.

SEARCH ENGINE OPTIMIZATION

Search Engine Optimization (SEO) is crucial for ensuring that your website is easily discoverable by search engines.

One of the most popular SEO plugins available is **Yoast SEO**.

Install

1. Go to **Dashboard > Plugins > Add New Plugin**.
2. Search for *Yoast SEO*.
3. **Install** and **activate** the plugin.

Usage

Yoast SEO	Install Now
Improve your WordPress SEO: Write better content and have a fully optimized WordPress site using the Yoast SEO plugin.	More Details
By *Team Yoast*	

After activation, Yoast SEO provides numerous options to enhance your site's SEO. For detailed guidance, refer to the online guide provided by the creator: https://yoast.com/wordpress-seo.

Permalinks

Customize Permalinks by navigating to **Dashboard > Settings > Permalinks** and selecting the **Post Name** option.

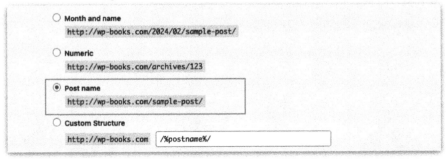

WWW or no WWW

www.site.com and **site.com** are two different URLs also for Google. How do you know if your website uses www or no www. Type in your address without www in front of it. If the site is loaded with www in the address bar choose a URL address with www. If you do not have www in the address and would like to have it, contact your web host.

Go to **Dashboard > Settings > General**.
At (URL) you'll see if you use www or not.

General Settings

Site Title	Carpe Diem
Tagline	
	In a few words, explain what this site is about. Example: "Just another WordPress site."
WordPress Address (URL)	https://wp-books.com
Site Address (URL)	https://wp-books.com
	Enter the same address here unless you want your site home page to be different from your WordPre

SEO rules

Familiarize yourself with SEO rules before proceeding. If you follow these rules, you increase the chances of your website being indexed properly by search engines. However, a plugin cannot guarantee this result; it only ensures that your content meets certain criteria.

Website title and pages

An important part of being found is your **site title** and **page titles**. These are displayed at the top of the browser and as link text in Google.

> https://wp-books.com › wordpress › basics
> **WordPress Basics - WP Books**
> This book describes how to install and configure a WordPress site. You will be introduced to the Dashboard (management environment). Then you will create content with Posts and Pages. Furthermore, you will learn how to create a Navigation and Social menu. And how to install and...
>
> WordPress Advanced   WordPress
> Binding: Paperback Distribution Form: WordPress - WordPress Basics - WP
> Book (print, print) Size: 145mm x 210m...   Books

▸ Titles may contain a maximum of 65 characters (including spaces).

▸ Include a call-to-action or ask a question.

▸ Position your most important keyword at the beginning.

Meta description

Another component to being found is the **description** of the site and underlying pages. This is displayed with Google below the title.

▸ Brief description of the site/page.

▸ Description may contain a maximum 150 characters (including spaces).

▸ Aim to increase Click-Through Rate (CTR).

▸ Use keywords.

▸ Full sentences are not necessary.

Meta keywords

Limit your selection to 10 keywords or keyword combinations. Although Google ignores meta keywords, other search engines do take them into account.

Usage

Avoid using the installation wizard; click **Skip**.

Next, go to **Dashboard > Yoast SEO > General**. In the screen, you'll see 2 tabs **Dashboard** and **Initial Configuration**.

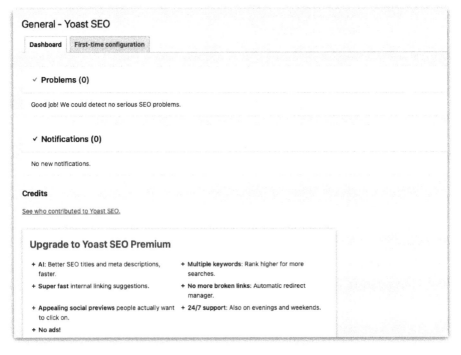

In this book, we will use the default settings.

If you want to use the advanced settings, go to **Dashboard > Yoast SEO > Settings**. There you'll find more information about the different features.

Using the **?** icon (bottom right) you can find more information about the various settings.

Pages and Posts

Navigate to **Dashboard > Pages** and select the **Front page**. At the bottom, you'll find Yoast SEO, where you can edit information like **title**, **description**, and **keywords**.

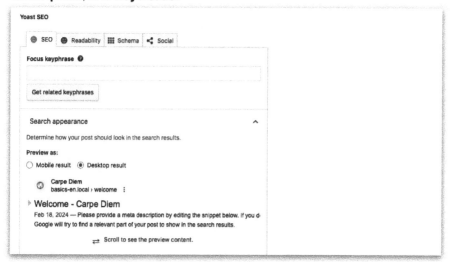

Use **Preview as** to visualize the result.

Adjust the **SEO title** and **Meta description**, indicated by a color bar reflecting SEO compliance.

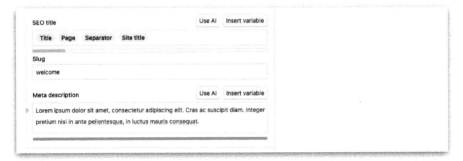

Place keywords in the **Focus keyphrase** section to enhance searchability. Utilize **SEO analysis** for insights on keyword optimization.

In the **Advanced** section, specify whether the page should be tracked by search engines.

It is good to indicate when a page should not be followed.

Click on the **Readability** tab for tips on improving page readability.

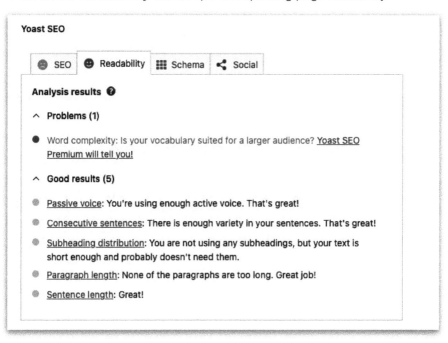

After entering SEO information, click the **Update** button.

A **green** light indicates compliance with
SEO rules; if **red**, review the instructions.

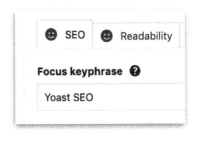

More SEO Tips

▸ Submit your website to search engines, e.g.,
 http://www.google.nl/intl/nl/add_url.html..

▸ Increase backlinks from other websites to improve visibility.

▸ Backlinks from high-ranking websites enhance your own pagerank.

▸ Create a list of relevant keywords for titles and subtitles, avoiding
 overuse.

▸ Incorporate relevant keywords into website text, using Header 2 for
 subtitles.

▸ Use textual content instead of image text.

▸ Give images clear names for better SEO.

▸ Ensure fast website loading speed:
 http://developers.google.com/speed/pagespeed/insights.

The Yoast SEO plugin enhances website indexing but doesn't guarantee
top-ranking. Don't solely rely on the traffic light; focus on quality content.
For higher visibility, consider Google Ads.

PRIVACY AND COOKIES

If you collect user data on your website, you are legally obligated to disclose this under European privacy law, known as the **G**eneral **D**ata **P**rotection **R**egulation (GDPR). The **GDPR** outlines regulations for the handling of user data.

To comply with GDPR requirements, including a Privacy Statement on your website is essential. This statement informs visitors about data collection practices and seeks their consent for placing cookies.

After a WordPress installation, a draft page titled **Privacy Policy** is created. This page serves as a template and is partially completed, ready for use.

To ensure compliance with GDPR standards, it's advisable to review competitors' websites to understand typical content included in privacy policies. Generally, a privacy policy should cover the following points:

▸ Purpose of data collection (e.g., for sending newsletters).
▸ Types of data collected (e.g., email addresses).
▸ Custodian of the data.
▸ Data publication status.
▸ Parties with access to the data (e.g., Google or Facebook).
▸ Data retention period.
▸ Data security measures (e.g., SSL certificate).
▸ Procedures for data deletion upon request.

To use the default **Privacy Policy Page** provided by WordPress:

Navigate to **Dashboard > Settings > Privacy**.

Click on the **Policy guide** tab.

Copy the provided section to the clipboard.

Go to **Dashboard > Pages** and select the **Privacy Policy** page.

Replace the text with the copied content and add any additional information as needed. Ensure the page is published.

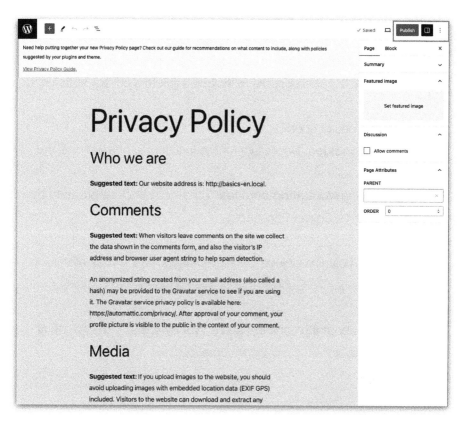

Place a link to the Privacy Policy page in the menu, footer, or sidebar of your website.

GDPR Plugin

With an GDPR plugin, you can inform visitors and request their permission to place cookies. It's also possible to include a link to a privacy statement.

There are two types of cookies:

1. **Functional cookies**: Necessary for the functioning of a website, e.g., WordPress cookies.
2. **Analytical** and **Marketing cookies**: Third-party cookies provided by platforms like Google or Facebook.

Tip: Many GDPR plugins include Cookie scanners, which work alongside tracking plugins such as Google Analytics or Facebook pixel plugins.

If you're unsure about the cookies used on your website, you can use an online cookie checker like : *www.cookiemetrix.com*.

Install

1. Go to **Dashboard > Plugins > Add New Plugin**.
2. Search for *Complianz - GDPR/CCPA Cookie Consent*.
3. **Install** and **activate** the plugin.

Complianz – GDPR/CCPA Cookie Consent   Install Now

Configure your Cookie Banner, Cookie Consent and   More Details
Cookie Policy with our Wizard and Cookie Scan. Supports
GDPR, DSGVO, TTDSG, LGPD, POPIA, RGPD, CCPA/C ...

By Really Simple Plugins

Usage

Go to **Dashboard > Complianz > Wizard**.

Follow the steps to configure the website. Under **General > Visitors**, specify the privacy law you want to comply with.

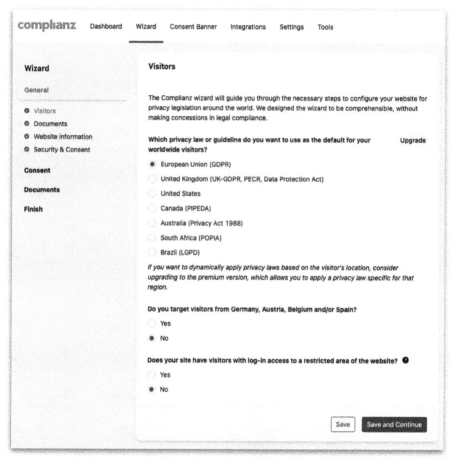

There are a few things that can help you during configuration:

▸ Use the question marks for more information.

▸ Important notifications are displayed in the right-hand column.

▸ You can submit a ticket for help.

Under **General > Documents**, specify the pages used for Cookie Policy, Privacy Statement, and Disclaimer.

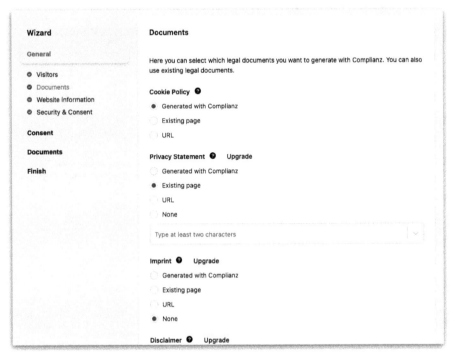

Under **Consent > Site scan**, scan the site for cookies.

The scan repeats monthly to keep the site updated.

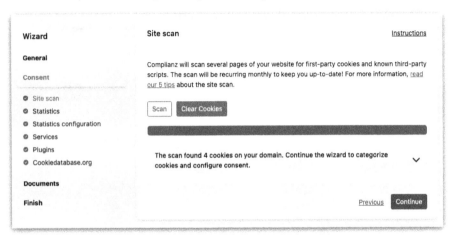

Under **Consent > Statistics configuration** , indicate if Google Analytics is used and enter the **Tracking ID**.

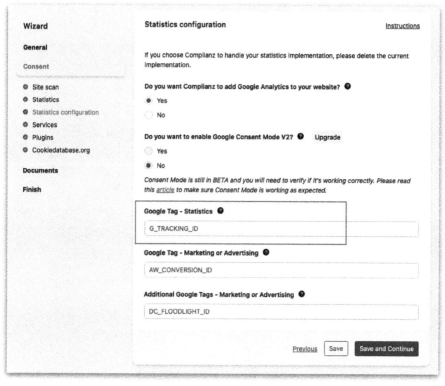

For more information, visit: *complianz.io/docs*.

Cookie banner design

Go to **Dashboard > Complianz > Consent Banner**.

Design the banner in this section.

Under **General**, disable the banner and manage the title, among other settings.

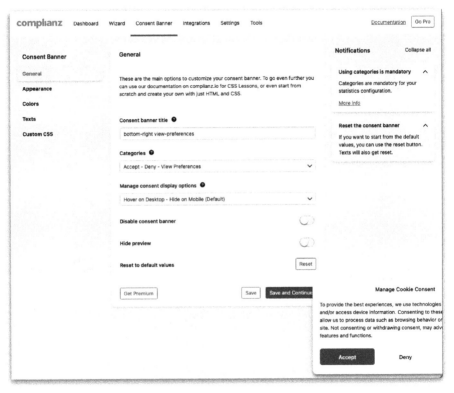

A preview is displayed in the lower right-hand screen.

Under **Appearance**, specify position and other visual settings.

Under **Colors**, adjust color and style.

Under **Texts**, customize text and message.

Under **Custom CSS** you can add additional custom CSS code.

SSL - SECURE SITE

Internet browsers warn visitors if a website lacks an **SSL certificate**. The address bar displays *Not secure*. After installing WordPress, your website does not have an SSL certificate yet. SSL stands for **S**ecure **S**ockets **L**ayer, creating an encrypted connection between the server and visitor.

With http**s**:// in the address bar and a **padlock icon**, you know the website is secure. You can obtain an SSL certificate by purchasing one or using a free certificate from Let's Encrypt.

SSL activation typically requires assistance from your hosting provider. In this example, we'll demonstrate the process using IONOS web hosting. However, if you're using a different hosting provider, you might need to follow a different procedure.

1. Log in to **IONOS** and navigate to **Domains & SSL**.

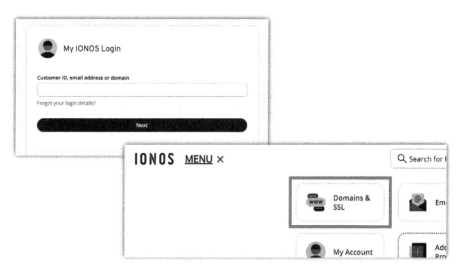

2. Click on the red **padlock icon** next to the domain you want to protect.

3. Select a certificate, such as **Free SSL Starter Wildcard**, and click **Activate Now**.

4. Choose the **domain** for which the SSL certificate should be issued.

5. In the **Change Usage** drop-down menu, select **Use with my IONOS website**.

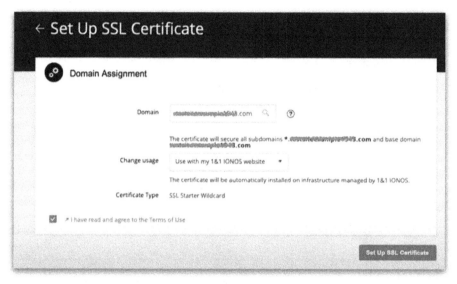

6. Verify and adjust your company details if necessary.

7. Read and accept the terms of use by checking the checkbox, then click **Set Up SSL Certificate**.

Activate SSL in Wordpress

After connecting the SSL certificate with a domain name, WordPress automatically detects its availability.

To activate SSL from WordPress:
Go to **Dashboard > Tools > Site Health**.

If the website is not using HTTPS, click the **Update your site to use HTTPS** button.

Review your website and address bar.

If updating doesn't work or you're using an older version, you can use the *Really Simple SSL* plugin.

Activate SSL with a plugin

Install and **activate** the *Really Simple SSL* plugin.

To activate SSL go to **Dashboard > SSL & Security**.

Then click **Activate SSL**! Review your website.

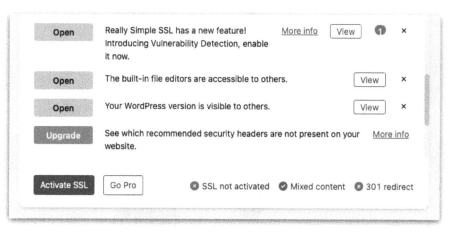

After completing, your browser's address bar will display a padlock icon.

HAVE FUN WITH WORDPRESS

Congratulations on completing this book and gaining the skills to set up and manage a WordPress site! You've covered a lot of ground, from setting up a local development environment to configuring WordPress, customizing themes, adding content, and enhancing functionality with plugins.

By exploring both the front end and back end of WordPress, you've gained a comprehensive understanding of how the platform works. You've also learned about important aspects such as security, privacy, backups, and search engine optimization, which are essential for maintaining a successful website.

Remember, WordPress is a powerful tool with endless possibilities. Keep experimenting, learning, and exploring new features and techniques to make the most out of your WordPress experience.

If you ever need assistance or have questions along the way, resources like the official WordPress website (wordpress.org) and its support forums are valuable sources of information.

Now, go ahead and have fun with WordPress! Let your creativity flow and build amazing websites that make an impact online.

WordPress Information:
wordpress.org
wordpress.org/support

ABOUT THE WRITER

Roy Sahupala, multimedia-specialist

" Multimedia specialist is just a title. In addition to creating multimedia products, I have been giving web design training for more than 26 years and continue to love it when people get excited by being able to do much more in a short time than they thought possible beforehand. "

After studying industrial design, Roy trained as a multimedia specialist. He then gained experience at several multimedia agencies. In 2000, he founded his own company, WJAC (With Jazz and Conversations), which specializes in creating multimedia products for various clients and advertising agencies.

Since 2001, in addition to his work, Roy has also been active as a instructor and has set up various web design training courses in cooperation with educational institutions.

WordPress books written by Roy Sahupala:

Explore WordPress books at *wp-books.com*.